SANDLOT FOOTBALL

Sandlot Football is a youth's story that recalls life in a simpler time and emphasizes the importance of family

By

George Washington Eaton III

TABLE OF CONTENTS

CHAPTER ONE
THE DELI STEPS

Before this summer day in 1948 my earliest teen years in West Philadelphia were mostly uneventful, not memorable, really- more like a blur. But it was this year and day where a number of events triggered major changes in my life for years to come.

The summer's vacation days were winding down to the final weekend and the long summer's heat wave wouldn't release its grip on life in the city. How hot was it? Like the old saw, "it was so hot you could have fried an egg on it," but it would have required an egg to test the saying. In the Eaton household with my parents, two brothers and two sisters a single egg couldn't be spared for a silly test.

This defining day had started like most summer days, when my buddies, Don and Bob, and two brothers, Si and Billy, and I were "hanging out" on the steps at Sam's Deli, the neighborhood's delicatessen. The city's street cleaning truck could be heard as it clanked its way around the 44th corner to head down Locust Street. Our gabbing was interrupted by the yellow monster that brushed its way toward us down the tree-lined Locust Street hill. Water spewed from the mechanism's nozzles and clouds of steam rose up from the sizzling asphalt. Large spinning brushes scattered bits of trash to the bordering curbs resurrecting foul odors of rotting refuse. Before the spinning, spraying, machine reached Sam's it lumbered past the vacant corner lot on one side of the street and the brick apartment house by the deli.

Sam's Deli was our neighborhood teenagers' hangout, our social meeting ground. Especially in the summer months, my brothers, friends and I met almost daily on the deli's steps to organize games and engage in all sorts of hi-jinx, "shoot the bull,"

1

kid around with the local girls, and pig out on Cokes, Pepsis, Nehis, hoagies, TastyKakes, and candy bars. We debated important matters like – "Well . . . what d'ya think we should do today?"

"C'mon Geordie–don't be a damned sissy," Bob taunted me.

"I'm not being a sissy! It's a lousy idea, and besides, it's too *doggone* hot."

To avoid confusion at home with my father, George, I was called Geordie. Even my friends and anyone I'd meet – I was Geordie. At age fifteen, I had lots of hair, sandy colored hair, but I believed I had to keep my hair long enough to comb over an annoying birthmark, a bald spot above my left ear. I envied my best friend, Don's crew-cut. I thought his burr was cool, because it didn't need combing and it was a snap to wash.

The sight of our group of guys gathered around the deli's steps, someone might think we were wearing the uniform of the day, but we were simply dressed for the summer heat in white Tee shirts, cut-off jeans or shorts, and Keds sneakers. Leaning against the deli's plate glass window and sipping from a bottle of Dr. Pepper, I was listening to Bob's latest idea for an adventure, but it sounded too crazy and risky.

Bob had to raise his voice to a shout, so he could be heard over the passing cleaning truck's racket. "For crying out loud guys, shut your traps and listen. Yeah . . . I know we've never done anything like this before, but I'm tellin' ya - the view from up there will be great."

Bob was a likable, outgoing, good-looking guy, but he liked himself – a lot. As Bob stood trying to sell his plan to our group, he pulled out from his rear pants' pocket a long, thin comb to caress his wavy, light brown hair's enormous pompadour. Bob had an ego that rivaled his pompadour, and he even fancied himself as his movie idol, Bob Cummings, an affable and glib "live for a laugh - die for a kiss" kind of guy.

2

We were in the midst of debating over the day's activity, but unanimity among our group was rare. This time, Bob was trying as hard as he could to promote his latest idea for an escapade. My two younger brothers, Simon and Billy, were sprawled across the deli's steps and more interested in wolfing down a package of Tasty Kake's chocolate cupcakes than buying what Bob was selling.

Simon, who we called Si, licked the last bit of chocolate off his lips, smiled, and asked, "Okay smart guy, do you have any idea *how* we can get up there?"

All heads bobbed up and down in agreement and craned forward for an answer.

Si was two years younger than me, but we weren't just brothers–we were pals. Everyone thought Si favored our father's features, a prominent nose and an angular face. My nose was shorter and I had a rounder face–more like our Mother's. Where my skin tanned in the summer's sun, Si's freckled and fair complexion would redden red and even flushed crimson every time he got agitated over almost anything.

His mouth, still full and smeared with chocolate cupcake, little Billy protested, "Geordie's . . . [mmmph] right! It's too hot and [mmmph] . . . I don't think I can climb up there!"

Bob snarled, "Who asked you to come anyway? Huh? . . . Gadget!"

My nine-year-old brother, Billy, was a feisty, pain-in-the neck, and a bothersome little kid to us older guys. I got to admit we didn't care that Billy didn't have friends his age in the neighborhood. We were just annoyed that he felt compelled to nose his way into everything us older guys tried to do. Because of his age, size, and a general irritant to all my pals, he'd been dubbed "Gadget." The Gadget moniker was a futile effort to control my youngest brother's oversized ego and discourage his incessant butting-ins. But, and a big but, we knew there'd be hell

3

to pay, if we called our little brother "Gadget" in front of our parents. Gadget was always Bill, Billy or William at home. Our little brother disliked intensely the nickname, but he had no choice but to tolerate "Gadget" on the street. The hated nickname only made him more defiant and more determined to stick with me and my friends.

With rocks in his pocket, Billy barely weighed fifty pounds. My friends kidded, "A stiff wind could blow him away," a joke that became a reality on a cold and windy wintery day. Billy had insisted on joining me on my newspaper delivery route. I actually enjoyed company, when I delivered the newspapers, even if it was my pesky little brother.

As we crossed 43rd and Locust Streets, a strong and sudden gust of wind roared down 43rd Street and lifted my little brother clear off his feet. He was blown across the street and plastered against the Divinity School's fence. The sight of Billy's flight across the street and being pinned to the fence sent me into hysterics. When Billy managed to peel himself from the fence, he started to wail uncontrollably. Even though my poor brother was crying his eyes out, I couldn't keep myself from laughing. My laughter surely didn't soothe his feelings as he leaned into the wind and struggled back across 43rd Street's wind tunnel.

"I'm goin' *home!*" He stomped and cried.

"Geez, Billy, don't go!"

"I'm [sob] going! You're laughing at me, so you can go by yourself!"

"Come back!"

To my disappointment my little brother didn't look back and marched away. I really wanted him along on my paper route, but the scene was just too funny. I continued to chuckle as I watched him head for home up the Locust Street hill and still crying. My amusement at Billy's expense came to a screeching halt, when I heard an ominous [flip] [flip] sound coming from my little red wagon that was loaded with newspapers.

I swallowed my last bit of "Ha," followed by an, "*Oh No,*" when I turned to see newspapers fly one by one out of my wagon into the wind and down the street. Before I could dive to stop any more papers from flying away, I had already lost a number of my customer's their delivery of the Philadelphia Evening Bulletin.

On the following weekend collections, I was asked, "Hey paper boy, what happened to my newspaper on Wednesday?' I pleaded complete ignorance, shook my head in disbelief, and raised my palms to the sky in wonder. "Gee I know I left the paper on your doorstep as always."

I knew if I told them that my brother flew across the street along with their newspapers, they probably wouldn't have believed me, or appreciated my excuse.

Rounding out our group at Sam's was my tallest and closest friend, Don, a tall, pug-nosed guy, with a blond crew-cut. Don was the nicest guy you'd ever want to meet, and the best friend anyone could ever have. As long as I'd known Don, he had suffered from asthma. Too often he found it difficult to breathe, and I hated to see him gasp, cough, pull an inhaler from his pocket, and breathe in its medication.

We had been good friends since Kindergarten at the Henry C. Lee school, and his parents treated me like their second son. His father was a retired dentist and the family lived in an attractive, gray stone and brick, three-story duplex at the corner of 44th and Spruce Streets.

Afraid he was losing his audience and sounding desperate, Bob pleaded, "Aww . . . c'mon guys, if we don't do it today, we'll never do it. There's only a few days left before we're back in school."

I still thought it was a bad idea, "Whew! It's hot as heck today and it sure sounds risky."

"Ya got a better idea?"

"No . . . I guess not."

Don said, "I'd be willing to give it a try [wheeze], but I might have to quit."

Billy whined, "No way! It's too hot and it's too high for me to climb."

Si's face turned its angry red and growled, "Welll . . . Gadget . . . then . . . for crying out loud - don't come with us!"

When it came to Billy, Si had a particularly short fuse and he had little patience with his younger brother. For some reason Si felt that it was the middle brother's job to keep an annoying Gadget in his place, but it sure wasn't easy.

"Not a chance! You're not leaving *me* behind!"

We were a group of relatively, well-behaved teenagers that stayed out of serious trouble. Since Sam's deli was our place to meet and organize games, some minor acts of mischief might be conjured up. Mostly harmless pranks included things like snowballing the Number 42 trolley on wintry days and nights, or placing tiny cap gun caps on the trolley tracks that ran up and down Spruce Street. When the trolley wheels bounced a little from the exploding caps, we would take delight in observing startled reactions from the trolley's conductor and his passengers.

Honestly, we weren't some kind of a trouble-making gang that purposely did devilish things. No, we were just a bored, little group of neighborhood guys that simply needed a few shenanigans to kill time and add a little spice to our uneventful urban lives. Especially during the long, hot, summer break, we had lots of time on our hands, and occasionally our time-killing activities became riskier and dumber. The escapade urged by Bob would prove to be among our dumbest.

With the sound of the deli door's opening, our group's discussion was interrupted by the appearance of the deli's proprietor. Sam, a short, slender, and balding man emerged from the deli. What little hair he had was a silvery gray. Sam, a friendly Jewish merchant, was forced to repeat an almost daily complaint. As he dried his hands on a long, white apron, Sam's tone expressed his exasperation:

"Boyce! Boyce! Boyce! How many times do I haff to tell you to move ofer and giff customers room to get in my store?"

Pretending to be annoyed with my brothers, I scolded them, "For crying out loud guys - move over! How many times does Sam have to tell you?"

Smiling up at me and without a word Si and Billy slid across the steps and away from the deli's entrance. All of us liked the Deli owner and we took his routine complaints in stride. On the other hand, Sam tolerated his deli being the focus of teenage activity, because most of us were good customers and spent almost all of our available dollars and cents in his shop. Sam's complaints stopped abruptly, when he spied the approach of a little, old, white haired lady. Instantly, his face transformed from a frown to a broad smile, just in time to greet his aged customer.

"Allo Missus Blackburn, itz so goot to see you again."

Sam took his customer by the hand and helped her up the deli's two steps. In opening the deli's door, a delicious, mouth-watering aroma of perfectly cured, Jewish corned beef and pastrami wafted into the street. Before the door closed behind him, Sam could be heard launching into one of his favorite songs, *Bay mir bistu sheyn . . ."*

The meeting resumed, and I felt compelled to say, "Okay! I-I-I . . . let's do it!"

Downing the last drop of my Dr. Pepper, I mimicked comedian Red Skelton's drunkard sketch, "[Burp!] Aaaah . . . good booze!"

By the time the cleaning truck's racket had reached the end of the block, we all agreed to join in the climb to the neighborhood's highest point, the Spruce Street apartment's garage roof. It was to be our Mount Kilmanjoro. I may have agreed to the newest caper, but I didn't like it, I thought it was stupid and risky, but I liked even less being called a sissy.

Even though I was the better athlete among my friends, I wasn't much of a risk taker. My timidity might have had something to do with the influence of my loving, but overly protective, Jewish mother, Fannie Sherman Eaton. My mother ruled the Eaton household and had to take charge, because of a necessarily absent, hard-working, Methodist father. George Washington Eaton, a city radio technician, who spent few waking hours at home. Because the city job barely supported his family, our father would plead for every available overtime hour and often worked 17 hour days. Our mother would often moan, "Oy, vai iz meir, we're forced to live from hand to mouth."

"I'm going too," Billy insisted.

I said, "Alright, but you'd better listen to what we say."

"Yeah – you'd better or else, you little bag of bones" Si warned, waving a finger in Billy's face.

Before things got out of hand, I stepped between my two brothers. "C'mon, lay off him Si."

The wrangling ceased, when Don said, "UH-OH here comes trouble!"

All heads turned to see trouble in the form of the two neighborhood bullies, Mickey and Ricky. They were four years older and considerably bigger than any one of us, and they took great pleasure in harassing younger kids in the neighborhood. The two lived around the corner on 43rd Street. "What are youse punks doin' here?" Ricky snarled, distorting his ugly, pock-marked face.

"Nothing, you'd be interested in," I muttered under my breath.

"What'd you say Jew boy? Mickey hissed. A shock of jet-black hair and a gaunt, narrow face completed Mickey's ugly, snake-like appearance. He had a mole on the end of his sharp. witch-like nose that made him even less attractive, if that was possible.

Mickey got in my face, "You're nothing but a little chicken." With that, he gave me a shove that sent me stumbling backwards.

"Why don't-cha pick on someone your own size!" Billy squeaked.

"Shaddup . . . Gadget! Shut your trap, you little pipsqueak!" Mickey hissed and spat at Billy's feet.

Regaining my balance and angry as hell, I knew that there was no way I could stand up against the two neighborhood bums. Either one of them could make mincemeat out of me. If I struck back, I'd get killed. If I sassed back, I'd get crushed. What did I do? I bit my tongue and clenched my fists. Too embarrassed to confront my enemies' looks of scorn, I turned my back on them and sputtered, "Uh . . . we gotta get going. C'mon fellas, let's go."

Without a moment of hesitation our little band tripped over each other in their haste to follow me. As we hustled away up Locust Street, Mickey shouted out, "You don't walk away from us Jew boy. Ya know we're gonna getcha!"

"Yeah, you'd better watch out ya little Jew punk," Ricky bellowed.

Don, walking beside me, said, "Don't let those jerks bother you. Just because your mother's Jewish, they call you a Jew, and what do they have against Jews anyway?"

"It beats the heck out of me!" I didn't sound too confident as I muttered, "They don't scare me."

Bob caught up to Don and me and said, "You know what? Those horses' asses ain't kiddin' 'round. I hear they joined up with the older guys on Ludlow Street."

Si said, "Jeez, Geordie, you don't want the Ludlow Street Gang after you."

There was no turning back, not even fear of the Ludlow Street Gang could we be swayed from our quest to climb our very own Kilmanjoro.

CHAPTER TWO
NO PLACE TO PLAY

If you hadn't lived in West Philly in the Forties and Fifties, it's probably difficult for some to understand how climbing onto roofs on a hot summer day could possibly be considered a fun activity for teenagers. But in those years growing up in the city streets of West Philly kids like us had few options for recreation or entertainment. Television was in its infancy, few homes had TV's, and the best television had to offer was Uncle Miltie's slapstick humor and a popular kiddies' show, Howdy Doody. We didn't have a television in our home, even though our electronic savvy, radio technician father was capable of building one from scratch, but he lacked the money to buy the necessary parts.

Radio was still the prime evening entertainment at our home. My favorite radio programs were comedies with hilarious, recurring scenes that guaranteed laughter every time: The sound of Jack Benny descending a long flight of steps and opening his creaking vault, or Fibber Magee opening his hall closet that created a noisy avalanche of God knows what spilling onto the floor. My family and I eagerly anticipated these repetitive happenings, and we still laughed every time, even though we had heard hundreds of times Benny's vault door creaking and the sound of all sorts of things tumbling out of Magee's closet. There were spooky, well watched programs like "The Shadow" that had an ominous intro, "Who knows what evil lurks in the hearts of men - the Shadow knows." That pretty much exemplifies how simple home entertainment was in those years, but it was all we had, and we loved it.

As for youth team games, there was no organized Little League baseball played on manicured baseball diamonds and organized Pop Warner football on grass covered football fields was only a dream to us. In the elementary school's playground, there were softball bases and lines painted on the asphalt field, one full basketball court, and a backboard mounted to the school's wall. Guys our age had to compete with the older high school basketball players for time on the basketball court. Because future basketball stars like Wilt Chamberlain came from other recreation-starved neighborhoods to play at the Henry C. Lee schoolyard's basketball court, our guys had scarce opportunity to play on the only court.

The YMCA on 52nd Street, a walk of about a mile, was the nearest swimming pool, but swimming at the YMCA wasn't much fun, because boys were required to swim in the nude. Once or twice in the summer, some of my pals and I would take an hour trek by the Market Street El and bus ride to a swimming pool in Springfield, a Philadelphia suburb. It was a long trip, but dressed in bathing suits we had a chance to flirt with suburban girls, and we were desperate enough to think it was worth the effort.

Without access to grassy fields of play, games on asphalt and concrete were created out of necessity. Our playground was the city streets, house walls, front steps, corner lots, alleys and backyards. While dodging traffic, two-hand-touch football was played on the Locust Street's hill near the deli, and one of my favorite games was stickball. In stickball, a box was drawn in chalk on the wall of the brick apartment house next to the deli. The batter stood by the box with a broomstick handle for a bat, and the pitcher hurled some kind of a ball, like an old tennis ball, from the pitcher's mound-the curb across the street. The box on the wall determined called balls and strikes. Groundballs past the pitcher were singles, doubles were fly balls hit across the street into the vacant lot, triples were balls hit against the side of the house that sat adjacent to the lot, and home runs were on the house's roof. A homerun ball hit on the house's roof caused only a brief moment of joy for the batter.

"WOW! ITS A HOMERUN!"

But reality quickly set in – that was the only ball, and the pitcher let the batter know it.

"Okay wise guy, where the hell are we gettin' another ball?"

Outs were recorded by three pitched strikes, and ground balls or pop ups caught by the pitcher. The stickball game usually ended when a home run was hit onto the house's roof, the apartment house's tenants would no longer tolerate the pitched ball pounding against the building's wall, or the house's owner grew tired of the extra base hits that rattled the pictures and mirrors on her living room and bedroom walls. We didn't understand complaints over our stickball games and considered the complainants as unreasonable by "Old.fuddy duddies."

Si and I often played another version of baseball, Step-Ball, on our home's front porch steps. Play began with a pink *Spalding High Bouncer* pitched by the "batter" against the concrete slab steps. Depending on exactly where the pitched ball hit the steps, the lively, pink ball would carom off the steps as grounders, pop ups and fly balls. Grounders past the "fielder" were singles, fly balls across Forty-Fourth street were doubles, triples were onto the porch across the street, and home runs were balls onto the porch roofs or higher.

Because Forty-Fourth Street happened to be the city's route for U.S. 1, going back for pop-ups, while looking out for traffic, added an element of excitement and a significant hazard for the fielder. The step-ball game usually ended abruptly, when residents across the street objected to balls bouncing onto their porches and against their front windows–more "old cranks."

The neighborhood girls joined us in some games like *Three Feet off the Ice*, a tag game played in the street in front of the deli and *King of the Hill*, another game of tag that was played throughout the back alleys and backyards. Unfortunately, no matter what game or where we played, someone would invariably appear to object to games in their yards, their home's wall, a lot, or even the street. Neighborhood kids realized that we were bound to trespass or annoy someone, no matter what we did or where we went.

Across the street from the deli, before the Acme market was built, retired Yellow Taxis were stored on a cinder lot. Rumor had it that the old taxis would be painted, and sold to unsuspecting buyers in the southern states and Mexico. Who knows? It was a rumor. A corner of the lot served as our softball field. It was a far cry from an ideal playing surface for any sport, since a fall on the lot's cinders surface made brutal brush-burns, and sliding into a base was an act of insanity. Adding to the poor field conditions, the lot's caretaker was a crotchety old man. When he was sufficiently annoyed by our trespassing, he'd limp out from his little guardhouse and shoo us off the lot.

"You boys, get off the lot! If ya don't, I'll call the cops on ya!"

"Calling the cops" was the ultimate threat, and we'd leave grudgingly and grumbling. Not to worry, we'd be right back on the lot the very next day and resume our softball game, only to be evicted again. This scenario was repeated so often that the old custodian would most often sigh in frustration, slump into his guardhouse chair, and allow our game to continue. But if a foul ball should bounce off one of the old taxis, that old man came to life. It was absolutely amazing to see how fast he could spring out of his little house and limp like an arthritic gazelle to capture the stray ball. I've never actually seen an arthritic gazelle, but I imagine the animal might have limped and loped something like that.

For us, there was no such thing as a new softball. All our softballs were minus their horsehide covers and wrapped in adhesive tape to prevent the yarn-insides from unraveling. But the loss of this poor excuse for a ball was devastating and summarily ended a game. We would beg so hard and long for the return of the ball that the old man would finally relent, but we had to promise to leave the lot and never come back. Needless to say, the game resumed on the lot the very next day. If we were chased again, not to be discouraged, my pals, brothers and I would reluctantly move on to another game in another place.

During World War II, my father didn't have a car and couldn't afford one. We relied on public transportation for travel around Philadelphia using the Market Street El, the Number 42 Spruce Street trolley, the Chestnut and Walnut Street buses, and downtown's Broad Street subway. About two times each summer, our family would travel to the New Jersey shore. When we went on these New Jersey beach excursions, Mom usually stayed home – she needed a break from managing a household and tending to what she called us, her "five little Indians."

Pop often mentioned that our family had some Blackfoot Tribe heritage, but I'm certain he was joking and only referring to the times his children arrived home from play with dirty feet. Besides, I had my heritage researched, and there was no reference to a hint of Native American in my saliva sample.

For transportation to the "Jersey Shore", we depended on our wealthy Uncle Will. Uncle Will was my father's sister Leona's husband. Our uncle was a wiry, leathery skin faced, kindly old cuss. His dark, rugged face was a result of hours in the sun and his mother's Portuguese lineage. His wealth came from his family's substantial real estate holdings. He was wealthy by any standard, and the man had a strong compulsion to stay that way. Our uncle didn't adhere to the "get a guy" theory of most wealthy individuals. If there was something to be done, he did it himself. With his old Negro assistant, Uncle Will walked the downtown streets of Philadelphia, collected rents, and made repairs to his properties. By Uncle Will's dress, a tattered shirt, old boots, and dirty coveralls, no one could ever identify him as a wealthy man. I'm sure he liked it like that.

Even our uncle's cars carried out the disguise. Uncle Will could have afforded to buy a brand new Lincoln or Cadillac every year, but he owned only three aged, broken down Lincolns that were never, I mean *never*, in running order. His Lincoln wrecks were stored out in the open on one of the vacant, weed-covered

14

lots that he owned. Each vehicle was unique in its particular stage of disrepair.

On beach day, my siblings and I were forced to stand by while Pop and our uncle slaved to assemble one running vehicle by pirating parts from the other Lincoln wrecks and scrounging other vital, rusting parts that were scattered around the lot. Miraculously, hours later, one Lincoln was declared operational. Pop, Uncle Will, and us five kids would pile into the car and head to the shore. Half the day had already been shot, and the car had barely enough gas to get us to and from our destination. Pop had little money for gas, even though gas cost only 10 cents a gallon in those years. Because we drove most of the way to the shore and back on gas fumes, the engine was turned off while coasting down hills and reignited at the bottom. On the way to the shore and back, the constant fear of running out of gas made the drive more stressful than necessary, and I'm almost certain that my nervous system still bears the scars.

By the time our group of climbers rounded the corner onto Forty-Fourth Street, I had shaken off Mickey and Ricky's threats. We were committed to our latest adventure – the epic climb to the garage roof. Still I fretted over the climb, "Oh well," I murmured to myself. "At least it's something to do." But as the day's events would unfold, I'd have been better off doing almost anything else, except maybe suicide.

15

CHAPTER THREE
THE LEAP

Our little band of climbers tramped down the tree-lined street of brick row homes. As we passed the middle of the block, I looked across the street and was relieved to see that my mother wasn't sitting in her command position on the front porch's rocking chair. I knew she would have been bound to ask me what we were up to, and I'd be forced to tell her something short of the truth.

Continuing our march up the street, we reached the plumber Blackwood's home. One would never suspect that the, lanky, and well-dressed Mr. Blackwood was a plumber until he began his work day dressed in coveralls and a crumpled fedora atop his head while puffing a long-stemmed pipe clenched between his teeth, and lugging a huge metal toolbox with a coil of copper tubing slung over his shoulder.

Our little group turned into the wide driveway that bordered the Blackwood's home. We marched down the driveway and began a cadence, "Left-right-left-right." I looked over my shoulder and was irritated to see that Bob, who had been so confident in selling this adventure, was lagging behind. Gone was Bob's cocky air. His eyes were shifting back up the alleyway, and each foot was reluctantly placed one in front of the other. It appeared the instigator had lost his enthusiasm for our mission-his idea.
"Hey Bob, how 'bout keepin' up!"
The young Romeo stopped to take out his every-ready pocket comb and primped up his pompadour that had drooped ever so slightly. Bob depended on his hair-wave to attract girls, but he refused to accept the fact that most girls our age were more interested in upper classmen in high school. Bob, being the

perpetual optimist, wouldn't accept defeat in the female chase and continued his quest to create the "woman-swooning-perfect-pompadour."

"Christ! Hold your horses, Geordie . . . I'm coming . . . *I'm coming.*"

Our climbing party came to a halt at Mr. Blackstone's garage, the first step in our planned ascent to the roof of the apartment house's garage. The plumber's garage door was closed, but through the garage window, all sorts of pipes, sheet metal, cans and piles of stuff could be seen.

"What a lot of crap," Don laughed.

"Yeah, how does he find anything in there?" Si chuckled.

Why was Bob hesitating? His fervor for adventure and the fire in his eyes had disappeared. It looked to me like he needed a stiff boot in the rear, and I growled, "All right, Bob, get your tail moving up."

"Ya know, Geordie, I'm wearing my best shorts and my mom will murder me, if I mess 'em up."

This was typical of Bob to come up with some outrageous things to do, convince everyone to go along, and try to back out at the last minute. Because Bob's mother worked long hours as a waitress, he was left to manage, not well, on his own. I believe he compensated for his lonely, boring home-life by dreaming up crazy things for us guys to do, like climbing onto the garage's roof. Bob's problem was he lacked the courage to follow through on the crazy things he instigated.

"What's that?! Bob, this was *your* nutty idea!"

"Yeah, Yeah, I know, but . . . ."

"No buts! Aww, forget it! I'll go first, but you'd better not chicken out. I thought it was a crazy thing to do - but now, it's just beginning to stink!"

I clambered ahead onto the plumber's garage roof. Boosting from the ground, Don and Bob helped me pull my brothers up. When Si and Billy were safely on the roof, I shouted, "Got em!"

17

Don hollered, "Geordie - how about it? Give us a hand – will ya!"

"Okay . . . keep your shirt on!"

I reached down to grasp a hand and help give each of my pals a lift up. After a few grunts and curses, we were all together on the plumber's garage roof, the caper's first stage. Still panting from the climb, we began to contemplate the next step.

Don struggled to speak between coughs and wheezes, "Geordie [cough], let's [wheeze] rest here a minute."

Seeing Don take several long breaths from his inhaler made me worry that he wasn't up for this gambit. Don wasn't the only one in his family that had a breathing problem. Because Don's father had contracted Tuberculosis, he had been forced to retire from a good dentistry practice in his office in the family's Spruce Street home. The dentist was a tall, slender and gentle man. He had been a heavy smoker, but his breathing limitations didn't cure his smoking addiction. The dentist would stash cigarettes all over the house like the actor, alcoholic Ray Milland, who in the movie, *The Lost Weekend,* squirreled away bottles of booze. It was a curious game, watching Don and his mother scour their home to locate the hidden cigarettes.

"Don, are you okay?"

"Yeah, Geordie . . . I'll be alright. I just need to [wheeze] catch my breath. By hook or crook, I'll make it." Don took out his inhaler and took another breath. Despite Don's bouts with asthma, he was determined not to allow it to stop him from joining us in any of our games and hi-jinks.

As soon as it appeared that Don began to breathe more normally, I was anxious to get on with it. "I'm sweating like a pig, but we gotta keep going." .

By now, sweat was pouring off Don's face "What's [wheeze] next, Geordie?"

"It should be easy from here. We can get up on that box and pull ourselves up to the garage roof."

"Geez, Geordie . . . We shouldn't be doing this!" Billy whined. "Mom and Dad are gonna kill us!"

Billy's complaint was met with an angry chorus, "Shaddup Gadget! Go on home NOW, if you want to!"

Stung by the groups' loud rebuke, Billy examined his shoes, shuffled his feet with embarrassment and blurted, "Like heck! I'm staying with you guys!"

Waving a threatening fist, Si snarled, "Then . . . *not* another *peep* outta ya!"

When it came to Billy, Si's temper had a very short fuse. As my brothers and I grew up, I had to step in as umpire, referee, arbiter, judge, intermediary on hundreds of squabbles between Si and Billy. If I hadn't intervened in my brothers' disputes, my littlest brother wouldn't have reached his ninth birthday, and certainly not have become a world-famous bio-physicist that he is today. It became painfully clear to me that Billy shouldn't have come with us, but it was too late to send him back down to the ground.

"C'mon Gadget, you can do it! Oh . . . Don . . . by the way - remind me why are we doing this?"

"Are you kidding? Ya know that we agreed that there was nuthin' much to do this afternoon, and this would be a good way to kill some time."

It tickled me to think that mu buddy took my teasing seriously.

"Okay, okay . . . I was just kidding. Is everyone ready to go up?"

I looked around at the circle of my nodding cohorts. Even Billy reluctantly signaled his agreement to continue the quest. Wasting no time, I spun around and shouted over my shoulder, as if commanding a troop.

"All right men! When we get to the top, I'll bet we'll have a great view of the entire neighborhood. Let's go! We can get to the garage roof easy from here."

One by one, with a boost here and there, we all managed to struggle up onto the roof of the apartment's garage. Once gathered on the high perch, our band of five stopped to scan over the lines of brick row homes along Forty-Fourth Street. From this vantage point, we found that the view made all our effort worthwhile.

"Wow - this is sort of neat up here! I can see my house on Spruce Street!" Don gleefully announced.

"Hey you guys! Take a look at the line of people over at Buddy's house," Si shouted.

"I know. I know. They're having a wake for Buddy," I mumbled.

"Weren't you gonna go to that thing, Geordie? I thought you and Buddy were friends?" Don asked.

"Nah . . . . I couldn't. I liked Buddy some, but I sure wouldn't be caught dead in that house."

Don smiled and said, "It's funny you said that – Buddy is dead in there."

"Okay, okay . . . I'm sorry I said that."

Two years earlier, in a rusted and dilapidated pickup truck, Buddy and the Pine family had arrived in our neighborhood from Oklahoma. Their truck must have died on the spot, right on 44th Street, two doors down from our row home. It was just our lousy luck that the house was available, and the migrant Pine family became our neighbors. Never seeing all the children together at one time, I had to take Buddy's word for it that he had only eight brothers and sisters. It seemed to me there must have been at least a dozen, but they were all so close in age and looked so much alike, it was hard for me to know their number and probably just as hard for the parents. Except for Buddy, his brothers and sisters were usually unwashed, often played in the street barefoot, and their clothes were well beyond hand-me-downs.

Of all the kids, I knew Buddy best, since he was the oldest, nicest, cleanest, and closest to my age. He had been killed a several days earlier. In skating down Locust Street hill, Buddy stumbled and fell beneath the wheels of a moving city's dump trailer. He was horribly crushed and instantly killed. Even though Buddy and I had been friends, the idea of seeing his corpse, in that house, was way too creepy for me. I had never been in his home when Buddy was alive, and I sure wasn't going in there when he's dead.

"Why did it have to be Buddy? Wasn't he the only good one in that whole darned family?" Don murmured.

"Yeah, why couldn't it have been that pain in the ass Peck?" Bob snarled.

Peck was a year younger than Buddy. His tangled, dirty, blond hair, freckled face and pug nose spelled nothing but trouble, and trouble should have been his middle name.

"Didja know that Peck has been hanging out with the Ludlow gang?" Bob asked.

I sniffed, "Yeah - he's been going around saying that he joined the Ludlow Street Gang. The little jerk thinks that makes him tough and we oughta be scared of him."

The Ludlow Street Gang consisted of one group of guys about our age and another group of their older brothers. They had a reputation for being a bunch of rough and tough Irish Catholic guys that delighted in terrorizing kids around the West Philly neighborhoods. The entrance to Ludlow Street was four blocks up 44th Street. It was a street of homes of hard working, blue collar, mostly Irish-Catholic families. Up to that time, except for Ricky and Mickey, we hadn't had a single encounter with the so-called Ludlow Street Gang. Our fears were fueled only by rumors, second to third-hand stories, and some tall tales designed to terrify. Peck's smart aleck attitude caused him to be universally disliked in our neighborhood, and his professed alliance with the toughies from Ludlow Street had further alienated him from our guys.

"Hey Geordie, is it true that Buddy's mom can speak to the dead?" Gadget asked.

I peered down on the crowd in front of the Buddy's house, "I don't know, but it sure looks like a lot of people think she can."

A crowd of mourners and spirit believers were gathered in a long line that spilled out of the house onto the street and halfway down the block. Some had come to pay their respects, but most were drawn to consult with the dead son's mother as soon as they learned of her reported supernatural powers. Buddy's death, a family tragedy, had miraculously and somehow bestowed upon the grieving mother with the ability to communicate with the dead through her poor, dead son's spirit.

Becoming antsy I wanted to get this whole climbing thing over with and began to walk further on the roof. "Forget about those nuts down there, I think we can get an even better view further up, and then we'd better head back down."

"I don't think I'm gonna like this," Billy whined.

Si growled, "C'mon Gadget - don't be such a danged baby,"

In a single file, the group followed me across the high, tarred roof. Unfortunately by taking my eyes off of where I stepped and looking further up the roof, I failed to notice the black, glass paned skylight, directly in my path.

CRACK! SNAP!

My right foot went down as the skylight's glass gave way, and the shock caused me to let out a loud howl,

"YEEOWW!"

Luckily, I had enough presence of mind to fall back as the broken glass sailed down to the garage floor below.

"JESUS!" bellowed Bob.

"WHOOOOA!" whooped Don.

"OH NOOOO!" Si screamed.

"MOMMEEE!" Billy cried.

Our screams might have reverberated as far as William Penn's statue atop City Hall, about thirty blocks away. For a moment, we looked like a scene from the silent Keystone Kops' movies - spinning our wheels, and arms and legs flailing in every direction.

Finally, we regained our senses and charged like a thundering herd's retreat to the edge of the roof. Si rushed to help Billy climb down to the first roof and from there they scrambled to the ground. Billy was crying hysterically as he followed Don, Bob, and Si in their frenzied cascade to the ground.

They were all frightened, but they hadn't broken the skylight - *I had*. When I had reached the garage roof's edge, I was panic stricken and all rational thought had evaporated. The descent the others had taken was too slow for my frantic state of mind. I thought of nothing, but getting down and *fast*. It was as if my life flashed across my eyes: Parental wrath – police arrest – corporal punishment – prison years. Driven by these horrible thoughts and a huge dose of terror, I leaped from the garage roof all the way down - down to the backyard below. Mercifully, my landing was softened by the garden's grass lawn. As soon as my two feet hit the turf, I instinctively rolled forward and came to a halt flat on my back. Because my legs and feet throbbed like crazy, I knew that I couldn't be dead. Several minutes passed while I lay on my back, content to wiggle my toes and relieved to be alive . . . until I heard a familiar voice.

"You [cough] . . . bird [wheeze] . . . bird brain!"

I could tell by the coughs and wheezes that it was Don, the first to reach my prone body.

"Are you alright?"

The others approached running and pulled up panting beside Don. I struggled to a sitting position. Before answering, I felt my arms and legs to make certain that there were no protruding bones. With the exception of my aching legs and feet, I really didn't feel too bad anywhere.

Hesitating for several seconds, my voice quivered, "Yeah...eh. I think so."

Don hollered down at me, "You're crazy! Why in hell did you jump?"

"I . . . had to . . . get down . . . fast."

As the pain eased, in scanning the group that surrounded me, I noted mixed expressions of curiosity, wonder, concern, and to my surprise, even a hint of respect. My brothers and pals seemed to hold some strange admiration for my desperate decision to jump. Never before had I done anything that might have even bordered on courageous. Concerns for my body and broken glass began to melt, replaced by a perverted sense of pride from *The Jump*. Hmm, I thought, maybe I should jump off a roof more often. I labored to stand up, wavered a bit, and stamped my feet to make certain that my legs and feet were still whole.

Billy gasped, "Gee, Geordie, you must have jumped a hundred feet!"

Bob laughed in saying, "He's nuts and you're nuts Gadget! That sure ain't no hundred feet, but damn - it was a lot!"

Gathering my senses, I realized that the broken skylight was big trouble and barely managed to croak:

"I, I, I . . . guess it was crazy. But . . . but . . . we'd better beat it before the cops come!"

It was no time for talking – it was time for splitting. We exited the backyard on a dead-run and galloped up the alleyway onto 44th Street. Tony, the neighborhood's Italian barber, was standing outside his shop, one door down from the alley. Fortunately for us, the barber was the sole observer of the stampede that spilled out from the alley onto the street.

"What's amatta with you boys? Why you run like that?" Tony shouted.

The barber knew from our frenzied exit from the alley and the terror in our eyes, something serious had just occurred.

"Is sometheen' chaseen' you?"

On this occasion, we weren't interested in a 50 cent haircut, or conversation with the neighborhood's favorite and only barber -

we were desperate to get to the sanctity of our homes as fast as our legs could carry us.

I shouted over my shoulder, "You didn't see us."

"I no see you?" Tony asked with an amused curl to his lips.

Don whispered as he passed the barber, "Right, you didn't see us."

The barber's thin mustache twisted up further with a beaming and white toothed smile, "That's-a- right, I heard you, but I no see you."

CHAPTER FOUR
OUR NEIGHBORHOOD

My West Philadelphia neighborhood was a unique place for a teen to grow and learn. The area was replete with interesting people, and benefited from a host of all the necessary societal elements for a fulfilling life.

Tony the barber was just one of the distinctive individuals that contributed to our neighborhood's melting pot of characters. Each morning, the tall and slender Italian barber would arrive at his shop, dressed in a black, Italian silk suit. In one hand he carried a little black, leather bag that contained his prized tools of trade: scissors, razors and combs. Tony's flowing white mane of perfectly coifed hair and delicately trimmed, razor thin mustache completed an almost regal appearance. Walking to and from his barbershop, he could have been mistaken for a successful physician on his rounds, or even a visiting Italian ambassador.

The Italian barber changed into his white uniform that was as immaculate and neat as his mirrored shop. During the day, he entertained himself and his customers by playing Italian operas on an old hand-cranked RCA Victrola. Tony had a fine Italian tenor voice. Without knowledge of the Italian language, everyone believed he knew the lyrics to every opera played. He may have faked the lyrics, but if he didn't really know them, it didn't matter. To his customers, Tony was as good as Enrico Caruso, the famous Italian tenor.

A Marilyn Monroe calendar, in all her bare splendor, became a prized attraction in the barber shop. One might ask, "Wasn't a Marilyn Monroe calendar out of place in these pristine surroundings?" The answer: Tony is Italian and Italian men admire and love women, especially Marilyn Monroe in the buff.

Besides, in those days, no self-respecting barbershop would be the same without nude, girlie calendars.

Our home on West Philly Forty-Fourth Street was in line with brick, three story, row homes and duplexes. Elm and Maple trees bordered both sides of the street. Most of the homes had tin roof covered porches that offered residents relief from the sun and heat on hot summer days and warm evenings. It was a time when homes lacked air conditioners, and oscillating fans and the front porch were the only means of escaping the sultry summer evenings. The front porch also served as the neighborhood's communication and social center. Neighbors chatted between porches, and friends would pause at the porches' front steps to pass on news and exchange pleasantries. The Row homes had small backyard gardens that were bordered by alleyways used for deliveries and trash collections.

The drug stores on the corners of 44th and 45th Spruce Street featured marvelous marble-top soda fountains where sandwiches and all sorts of ice cream and soda concoctions were served.

When I was only ten years old, my first job was making home deliveries from the 44th Street's drug store's pharmacy. At times, I helped behind the counter to serve sodas and ice cream cones. Technically, I was too young for soda fountain work, but the owner and his wife allowed me to assist in preparing simpler concoctions of vanilla cokes, cherry cokes and ten cent ice cream cones. I wasn't permitted to handle more sophisticated stuff, like sundaes, banana splits, milk shakes and sandwiches.

Homes in West Philadelphia were a combination of distinctive neighborhoods west of the Schuylkill River that differed in ethnicity and social strata. My 44th Street neighborhood was unique in its mix of social levels, from the debutante's socialite family that lived in a large, brick duplex on the Spruce Street's corner to "the shady lady," who lived with her little son in an apartment on the opposite Locust Street corner.

The Pines family lived in the middle of the block, two doors down from our row home. We were fortunate that a nice old couple lived between our two houses, which acted as a sound buffer from the bedlam emanating from the Pines' parents who dressed their children poorly and were oblivious to the clutter in their backyard.

The prestigious University of Pennsylvania's campus centered at 36th and Spruce Streets was only a short, eight, city blocks away. Our little community benefited from an academic element provided by the number of Penn's students and faculty that lived in our neighborhood's houses and apartments. Our main path to the university was east on Locust Street and past the wooded, Protestant Episcopal Divinity School's grounds that covered an entire city block. In my younger years, kids from the surrounding area came to sled down the school's snow covered hills. Invariably, the sledding fun would come to a halt, when a white collared faculty member emerged from one of the gray stone buildings to demand that everyone leave the premises. If the minister felt he was being ignored, he'd issue the deadly threat, "I've called the police!" That one got our attention and everyone scattered, but we would return to sled the hills the very next day.

Continuing on Locust Street, the homes between 41st and 40th Streets was a bit of an oddity due to the fact that a number of colored families lived in the block. It was unusual, because few colored families lived south of Market Street. Even stranger, white residents tolerated this single block of "colored" families just around the corner. If West Philadelphia's history held true, a single colored family's move around the corner onto 41st Street might have initiated another "White Flight," like the "change" that had occurred north of Market Street, many years earlier.

Notably, that same isolated block of colored families produced an Eddie Bell, a West Philadelphia High football's City All Star, All American end at the University of Pennsylvania, who went on to star for the NFL's Philadelphia Eagles. Market Street and the Market Street El represented a demarcation line between white and colored neighborhoods, a line that generally held during my years in West Philly.

Within ten city blocks, not more than a mile from my front door, it was an easy walk to Franklin Field on Thirty-Fourth and Spruce Streets where crowds of 75,000 watched the University of Pennsylvania play major college football teams. It was a time that Penn dominated other Ivy League teams and Al-Americans like Chuck Bednarik and Eddie Bell played big-time football for Penn. During the war the Army's fabulous football stars, Mr. Inside and Mr. Outside, Doc Blanchard and Glen Davis thrilled crowds at the Army-Navy games. The Penn Relays was another important sporting event held annually at Franklin Field.

Across the street from the stadium, my siblings and I spent many summer days in the University Museum's Junior Guide program. We were given pictures of museum relics and artifacts that were displayed throughout the museum, and we would scour the museum to identify each pictured item's location. One area in the museum exhibited a marvelous replica of an Egyptian tomb. Whenever I entered the tomb, my skin crawled for fear that a mummy would rise out of a sarcophagus and wrap shriveled, bony hands around my little neck.

Less than a block from the museum, down Thirty-Fourth Street, the city's Convention Hall hosted all types of activities, including national political conventions, performances by famous entertainers like Liberace, professional and collegiate basketball games, track meets, sports shows, and flower shows. Because of my mother's love for flowers, she never missed the annual flower shows. One of my father's jobs was to operate Convention Hall's sound system, which provided my siblings and me the opportunity to attend events that we otherwise couldn't afford.

Pop would say to me, "C'mon sunshine, I'm on my way to Convention Hall for a basketball game."

I loved basketball and I'd be thrilled to tag along with my father into the stadium's back door, carrying a microphone cable to make me look official. The guard at the door surely knew I was too young to be a city worker, but he winked at my father and let me pass with a smile. From the Hall's balcony, first row, and center court seats, my brothers and I got to see a lot of exciting college and professional basketball.

The Philadelphia Warriors, with "Jumping Joe Fulks," played in NBA double headers against the likes of the famous George Mikan and his Minneapolis Lakers. At the time, the talented and entertaining Harlem Globetrotters was only an opening entertainment for the Warriors' game, even though the Globetrotters featured the legendary Goose Tatum and the amazing ball handling wizard, Marques Haynes.

Today's basketball players have an array of shots, but in the late 1940's, each Warrior player appeared to have a single, signature shot: Forwards "Jumping Joe Fulks" popularized the jump shot and Howie Dallmar had a patented, flourishing, two-handed-double-pump-underhand-layup. The guards, Angelo Musi was deadly with a two-handed set shot while George Senesky stabbed a one-handed set shot. The center, Ed Sadowski worked the key with a sweeping hook shot.

I enjoyed college basketball doubleheaders and its stars just as much. Temple, St. Joseph, and Lasalle universities played most of their home games at Convention Hall, and I was privileged to see some of college basketball's All American greats: St. Joseph's George Senesky, Temple's Bill Mlkv ("The Owl without a vowel"), and Lasalle's super star Tom Gola. Bill Mlkvy's favorite shot was from a spot near the sideline, just inside the half-court line. It must have been well beyond the NBA's current three point line, and he was deadly from that distance.

A neighborhood commercial center was up the hill on 45th Street, between Locust and Chestnut Streets. In walking up the Locust Street hill to 45th Street, one of my fondest memories was the delicious aroma of frying fish and french-fries that spilled from a little seafood shop near the 45th Street corner. Across Locust Street from the seafood shop, the Model Laundry, produced sounds of steam and presses that added to the clamor of the busy shopping district around the corner on 45th Street.

Residents from blocks around shopped at the Penn Fruit market, Woolworth's Five and Dime, Pep Boys auto supply, and a local hardware store. A bank stood on the Walnut Street corner across the street from Don and his family's Methodist church.

The local Commodore movie theater was just around the corner from my home at 43rd and Walnut Streets. The Commodore was our regular Saturday afternoon destination to see just released, great films like *It's a Wonderful Life, Treasure of the Sierra Madre,* and *All the King's Men.* At Saturday matinees I cheered at the Oaters, cowboy movies, when the white-hat-heroes appeared and lustily booed the black-hat-villains.

Still, within reasonable walking distance, 52nd Street was a larger shopping district, with theaters, all types of shops, and the marvelous Horn & Hardart's Automat under the Market Street's El stop. As a boy, my happiest, though infrequent dining-out experiences, was putting nickels into an Automat's coin slot and drawing out from the windowed compartment a little brown pot of the world's best tasting baked beans, not to mention the enjoyment of savoring H&H's rich hot chocolate dispensed from an ornate, silver spout.

Another neighborhood landmark was America Bandstand that began televising a teenage dance show in September 1952 from the WFIL studio on Market Street, between 45th and 46th Streets. My little brother, Billy, aka Gadget, eventually grew up in time for me to see him dance the *Mashed Potatoes* on TV's Bandstand.

Next door to WFIL's studio was the venerable Philadelphia Arena, which featured Ramblers' ice hockey, rodeos, and wild professional wrestling matches.

Because my buddies and I couldn't afford a ticket to the Arena, we were sometimes successful in sneaking in the Arena's back door. As a young interloper I was fascinated to see some amazing things like the rabid and raucous wrestling fans, a hockey goalie that took a puck in his unprotected mouth (Hockey players didn't wear helmets and goalies didn't wear masks in those days), and the cruel way the rodeo's bulls were strapped over their testicles to make them buck. Because of that cruelty to the bulls, to this day I can't stomach rodeos.

Our elementary school, Henry C. Lea, was on Forty-Seventh and Locust Streets across the street from West Philadelphia High. We were fortunate that education, from kindergarten to college, was within easy walking distance. Around the corner from 44th Street, on Spruce Street, our neighborhood's doctor and dentist had their homes and offices together in gray, stone duplexes. Unlike today, family doctors made house calls. Further, it was only a short walk to reach three major hospitals and churches of practically every denomination. All in all, my West Philly neighborhood was an exceptional place to grow up – all desires and needs in education, shopping, entertainment, sports, religion and medical needs were satisfied within a mile radius.

It should be noted that about forty years before I walked up Locust Street's rows of homes to West Philly High, my teenage mother had walked through an undeveloped area and woods to attend the very same school.

But at this moment, we weren't pursuing any of the fine attributes offered in our neighborhood – my brothers and I were desperate to escape to our home's sanctuary and as far away from the broken skylight as we could get.

CHAPTER FIVE
SAFE AT HOME

Without stopping to look in either direction for oncoming traffic, I ran ahead of my brothers in a mad dash across the street on a beeline for home. Throwing caution to the winds, we could have been killed crossing the busy street like that - my luck was running bad, just not that bad. I ran ahead of my brothers up the concrete slab steps that led onto our front porch. Before entering the front door, I turned to my brothers, clenched my teeth, and gave them my best Jimmy Cagney impersonation.

"Listen you guys . . . you better not squeal on me to Mom and Dad."

Breathlessly, Billy struggled to say, "Don't worry [pant] Geordie, I [pant] won't say anything."

Wiping large beads of sweat off his brow with an open hand, Si took a couple of deep breaths and gasped, "Me neither."

Opening the front door, my brothers and I padded over the red tiled vestibule to enter the first floor hallway. I spotted Pop buried into his favorite lounge chair in the corner of the living room and fast asleep. The sight of him asleep in his chair wasn't unusual, but it was strange that he was home this early in the afternoon. Jeff, our family's pet, a brown, black and white Beagle came scampering down the hallway to greet us. As if he was on a pogo stick, Jeff excitedly bounded up and down.

We desperately waved him down, "Shhhh Jeff!"

We were lucky that Jeff didn't trumpet the Beagle's notable howling card, a sound that could wake the dead and certainly rouse my father. Jeff was excited to see his pals and couldn't resist awarding us with his normal enthusiastic greeting. He jumped on each of us while attempting to lick as much bare skin as he could reach with his Beagle tongue. Sweaty and salty skin was Jeff's absolutely favorite flavor.

The Beagle had become the family pet after a long line of stray alley cats that Si's twin sister, Betsy would drag in from the street or alley. Our sister loved her cats, but they all turned out to be "losers" in the alley's catfight arena. It was painfully obvious that her cats had lost every battle at night in the alleys. Elmer, Betsy's last feline pet, was "the cat that broke the camel's back." One fateful morning, Betsy entered the back door weeping and carrying the remains of her pet cat, Elmer. Elmer was a reasonable facsimile of a cat, but only from the neck down.

Mom cried out, "Oy Vai iz mir, Betsy! Don't bring that thing in the house!"

Most people familiar with felines probably may have recognized that piece of mangled fur and flesh as a cat, but the problem in identifying Elmer was his missing features. An ear had been torn off, a gaping gash down his nose, one eye was swollen, and the other eye was missing. Elmer was half dead and Betsy was hysterical. It took a lot of convincing, but Elmer was put to sleep and Jeff the Beagle was brought in to save the day. Jeff helped appease Betsy and thankfully, permanently replaced the "loser cats." Instantly, Jeff commanded affection from the entire Eaton household.

Jeff's noisy welcome worried me and I had to warn my brothers, "Whatever you do, don't wake up Pop," I spoke to my brothers in a deliberate and hushed voice.

It wasn't good to wake our father. When the family's "bread winner" came home after a routine, double-shift day he would collapse into his recliner and pick up a piece of his favorite reading material. His reading material consisted of radio and electronic magazines, Calculus textbooks, or some other mathematical text. Pop had an incredible thirst for technical knowledge, but fatigue would catch up with his reading. He would soon fall fast asleep and snore loudly.

After a full day repairing police radios or operating sound systems, Pop came home to eat dinner, then leave to work another four or five hours on a sound system job at Convention Hall, City Hall, or Municipal Stadium. In working long days almost every day, you wouldn't think he'd be a light sleeper, but the slightest sound could startle him up to a standing position, shouting at the top of his lungs.

"WHAT WAS THAT NOISE?"

On occasion my father used his chair for something other than reading and sleeping. He wasn't a devout Methodist, and Pop enjoyed a good bawdy joke as much as anyone. Without much encouragement, my father, while sitting in his chair, would perform for an audience his version of a quotation from the scriptures:

"He, who sitteth upon a tack, shall rise and shout the name of our lord and savior – JESUS CHRIST!"

With the shout of "Jesus Christ," my father, the performer, would leap to his feet, as if he actually had sat on a tack. He enjoyed performing this one-act play, and no matter how many times his audience had witnessed Pop's performance, everyone would laugh along with him.

Still shaken from our rooftop experience, Si whispered, "I'm going up to our bedroom until things cool off."

"Me too," Billy said on his way up the stairs, following on Si's heels. He turned and added, "Geordie, call us when the coast is clear."

Even though I felt as rattled as my brothers, the mouthwatering aromas emanating from the kitchen were too enticing and lured me down the hallway. Entering the brightly lit kitchen, I saw my mother and Tante Hinda, my Jewish Aunt Anne, chatting at the family's formica topped, kitchen table.

Our home's kitchen walls and ceiling were painted a vivid yellow. The speckled, well worn, linoleum floor had seen better days – years ago. The kitchen was equipped with an old, stained porcelain sink, a hand-me-down refrigerator that had replaced an icebox several years earlier, and a very old gas range of unknown origin. The room itself snugly accommodated a table that sat the family's seven at dinner, but this was our family's kitchen, and we loved it.

I did my best to mask my nervousness from the misadventure by forcing a cheery announcement.

"Hi, Mom something sure smells good! What're we having for dinner?"

"Hello, bubeleh. We're having meatloaf and something special for dessert. Did I hear your brothers come in with you?"

"Yeah, they just went upstairs."

"Geordie, why are you perspiring so much?" A curious and always perceptive Tante Hinda asked, raising her thick eyebrows.

My Jewish aunt was as short as her sister, but very slender, unlike my pleasingly plump mother. Unfortunately, my mother and aunt inherited poor eyesight and both wore glasses with equally thick lenses.

"I was running a little."

Tante Hinda and her husband lived in our third floor apartment. She was childless and treated us kids as if we were her own. Her husband, Uncle Nathan, had been forced to retire from his tailoring profession as a cutter, blinded by Glaucoma. This infliction made him an extremely morose person, in stark contrast to my aunt's cheerful disposition. It was amazing to me how my aunt could maintain her high spirits living with a man that brooded all day. Before my uncle's forced retirement, Tante Hinda and Uncle Nathan lived comfortably on a skilled cutter's income in a beautifully furnished row home about a mile away in another West Philadelphia neighborhood.

36

"We're going to have dinner in a couple of hours. Your father has to work again tonight, and I want to have dinner for him before he needs to leave."

"Oh . . . okay . . . Mom." I just need a drink of water - I'm staying in."

"Bubelah, do you feel all right? Come over here – let me feel your forehead." My mother gently put a cool palm of her hand on my damp forehead. "Hmm . . . you don't have a fever." With that pronouncement, Mom pulled my head down further to donate a peck on my brow.

"Sure. I feel fine. I wanna stay in and read something. I think I'll go sit in the living room and read a book. Boy, things sure smell good!" At the sink, I stopped to fill a glass with water and took several, long, thirsty swallows.

"I've made something special for dessert. Go ahead and read while I chat with your Aunt."

Instead of walking back up the hallway, I chose the path through the dining room to reach the living room. Our dining room was a little cramped with large pieces of furniture: A glass-front china closet displayed my mother's treasured set of Spode china. A long dining room table almost filled the room, and a ponderous credenza displayed a few family heirlooms and a prized, brass, Russian samovar.

The adjoining front living room had a warm, comfortable feel, like an old shoe. Pop's throne, the recliner, commanded one corner and an antique, drop-top secretary stood in another corner. Over the tile surrounded fireplace, brass works of art were displayed on the mantle's shelf. A well-worn, plush sofa faced the fireplace, and a drop-leaf table stood in front of the room's large, plate glass window. The window invited in the light from the morning sun's warming rays and looked out onto the front porch and street.

Still worrying over the broken skylight, I tried to calm myself by slumping onto the sofa to read a book. I sank comfortably into

37

the sofa, a piece of furniture that had experienced a number of rehabilitations and sagged a bit in the middle. No sooner had I turned a page I was jolted to my feet by a loud noise.

CRACK!

Something hard had struck the front window. As expected, Pop was shocked from his nap and shot upright in his chair.

I leaped to the window and spotted Mickey and Ricky walking away up the street and laughing.

"WHAT IN THE HELL WAS THAT?"

"I think it was the punks, Mickey and Ricky. I see 'em going down the street laughing. They must have thrown a rock or something at the window."

"WHAT . . . THOSE LITTLE BASTARDS!"

Fired up with rage my father catapulted out of his chair and charged from the living room like an angry bull, out the front door, and down the porch steps two at a time. I followed on Pop's heels out onto the porch, but I hesitated at the top of the porch steps. I'm not sure why I hesitated to follow my father in his race after Mickey and Rickey, but I was surprised by the speed of his dash up the street in hot pursuit of the two hoodlums. He had never played sports, but his speed to intercept the two bums must have come close to Jesse Owens' 1936 Olympic record of 10.3 seconds in 100 meters. Before they knew what hit them, Pop caught up to the young hoods, grabbed Mickey by his collar and spun him around. Then, with his other hand lifted Ricky off the ground, a well-built eighteen-year-old, and shook him until his teeth rattled.

"WHAT IN THE HELL DID YOU TWO THINK YOU WERE DOING?!"

Mickey blurted out, "You're crazy – we ain't done nuttin!"

"Like *hell!* You must've thrown something at my window."

"Let us go old man!" Mickey shouted.

As he wheeled around to face Mickey, Pop dropped his limp partner in crime. Then Mickey was picked up by the scruff of his neck and Pop shook the writhing teen.

"You're nothing but a couple of *punks!* If you ever try anything like that again, I'll do more than shake you."

Pop dropped a thoroughly shaken and sufficiently stirred Mickey and put an exclamation point on his warning by jabbing a finger hard into Mickey's chest. For good measure, he gave Ricky a hefty shove, turned, and strode back to our porch.

From my position of safety, as Pop headed toward me, I saw Ricky and Mickey glaring at Pop and me. Obviously, they weren't happy and mouthed curses and threats in our direction. If I could have read lips, I might have been better prepared for what would come later. I could only imagine what the two were saying, and I was sure it wasn't good.

As my father climbed back up the porch steps, I couldn't resist saying, "Gee Pop, you did great!"

"Do you know why those two punks would have done something like that?"

"I'm not sure, but they were bothering us guys earlier today. Ever since they joined the Ludlow Street Gang, they think they can get away with anything."

"Ludlow Street Gang, you say?"

"Yeah, they're a bunch of older, tough guys . . . over on Ludlow Street."

"Well, I don't care who they are or where they're from – that'd better be the last of them."

Following Pop back into the house, I found a new appreciation for his strength and broad shoulders. The way he manhandled Ricky and Mickey was inspiring. In growing up, my brothers and I had felt samples of our father's power through a number of stinging, disciplinary spankings, but this was different.

Returning to his chair in the living room, Pop was still fuming. I fell back into the sofa and returned to my book, but I couldn't concentrate on a single word. Looking over at my father, I saw him pick up a radio magazine, but he was clearly too upset to read. Pangs of guilt spread over me for not supporting him against my mortal enemies. Then, I began to wonder what would be Mickey and Ricky's next bad act. There was sure to be one.

CHAPTER SIX
THE ODD COUPLE

My parents, George Washington Eaton and Fanny Sherman may have been looked at as an unusual union, because of the differences in religion, education, and social strata, but it could not be denied that they were anything but exceptional people. It was only odd that two people, who came from completely different walks of life, could discover each other, fall in love, and agree to marry. What the two had in common was an incredible intelligence, a sharp sense of humor, and a mutual respect and affection for each other.

Fanny was a London born, college educated, Rabbi's daughter from a comfortable Jewish neighborhood in West Philadelphia. She graduated from Temple University and received her Master's degree at the University of Pennsylvania.

George came from a family of Methodists and he was a very bright man with only a high school education. He grew up in a blue collar, Italian section of South Philadelphia where his mother baked bread to help support the family. Because the Eaton family couldn't afford college for George, the young man became a radio operator, "Sparks", in the merchant marine.

Shortly after William Penn arrived in Pennsylvania, The Eatons migrated from Radnorshire, Wales and settled in Pennsylvania's Philadelphia area. My father's grandparents, Ananias Eaton and Sarah Hatfield Eaton were engaged in a "medicine man" styled business. From a wagon the family sold an elixir that was guaranteed to cure any disease or ailment from gout to influenza.

Albert, the Eaton family's eldest son, was sent to college and medical school so that he could endorse the elixir's healing

41

properties. Once Dr. Albert Eaton became a physician in Philadelphia, his medical ethics wouldn't permit him to support the exaggerated claims of the Eaton family's elixir, which ultimately led to the end of the family's enterprise.

The family's younger son, the first George Washington Eaton, my grandfather, wasn't afforded the benefit of a college education like his brother Albert, an omission that was to be repeated for his own son, my father. My grandfather, son of Ananias Eaton and Sarah Hatfield, became an iron molder by trade and married Adelaide Allen, daughter of William H. Allen and Eleanor Wagner.

My grandfather's iron molding business must not have been prosperous, since Adelaide, my grandmother was forced to open a bread bakery business from their South Philadelphia home's kitchen. A young George Washington Eaton Jr, my father, delivered his mother's bread by horse and wagon in all kinds of weather throughout the city. One of my father's painting depicted him as young boy leading a horse and wagon in a snow covered street.

While a wealthy aunt financed a college education to my father's sister, Leona, the aunt inexplicably overlooked her nephew's potential. As Leona nurtured a beneficial relationship with the wealthy aunt, my father was too busy delivering bread and studying radio technology to cozy up to the elderly aunt. Even though he was denied the opportunity for a college education, George possessed an innate intelligence and inquisitive mind, and at an early age developed a keen interest in radio. As a teenager he joined the merchant marine and became a ship's radio operator.

In one of my father's voyages, he visited Paris and the young radio operator managed to master one particular discourse in the French language. With or without encouragement, my father would happily recite to an audience of friends and house guests a mini play. The male's part Pop would speak in a deep voice, and the female's part in a falsetto voice:

"Bon jour Mademoiselle."

"Bon jour Monsieur."

"Voulez vous couche` avec moi ce soir?"

"Oui monsieur."

"Combien?"

"Dix francs."

"BON MARCHE', ALLONS!"

This one act play drew big laughs from his audience, and prompted Pop to repeat it every chance he got, with or without encouragement.

My mother, Fanny, was the youngest child of Rabbi Simon Sherman and Betsy Sherman. The family included a brother, Abraham, and two sisters, Leah and Anna. The Sherman family had escaped a Russian Pogrom in Riga, Latvia and settled for years in London, England where Fannie was born. When Fannie was eleven, the Sherman family moved to West Philadelphia to join relatives that had migrated earlier. On 39th Street and Powelton Avenue, Rabbi Sherman founded the Beth Tefillah Israel synagogue.

Fannie was a precocious and intelligent child. The first day that she and her mother traveled on a Philadelphia trolley, little Fannie was amazed by the number of Negro passengers on the trolley, an extremely unusual sight for the little English girl. She turned to her mother and exclaimed in a decided English accent, "Oh mother, look at all the Niggers!" Trolley passengers were amused by the little English girl's exclamation and roared with laughter. My mother enjoyed repeating this story not as sign of prejudice, but as an amusing example of her childhood innocence.

A stellar scholar in school, Fanny became the only child in the Sherman family to be afforded a college education. After graduation from Temple University, she went on to graduate school at the University of Pennsylvania, and as fate would have it, she met Leona Eaton. To the Sherman family's chagrin, "the shikseh," Leona, introduced beautiful and intelligent Fanny to her tall, handsome, brother and "goya," George.

After receiving her master's degree, Fanny began teaching Latin in the Mays Landing, New Jersey's high school, but her move to New Jersey didn't stop an ongoing relationship with Leona's brother, George. When the Sherman family learned of their youngest daughter's continued interest in George, they tried everything to discourage their relationship, but their protests failed. I can only imagine the angst in the Sherman family, "Fanny, if you must, just be friends with him, but whatever you do . . . don't marry that Goya! There are plenty of nice, Jewish boys to marry!"

In the beginning of the 1929 "Crash", after dating for five years, and turning a deaf ear to her family, Fanny Sherman eloped with George Washington Eaton to Elkton, MD. The moment Rabbi Sherman learned that his youngest daughter had married "The Goya," he disowned her. Fanny remained estranged from her family until she became pregnant with her first child. At that point, Rabbi Sherman and family could no longer bear to ostracize their youngest daughter and their expectant grandchild. In his own synagogue and against his principles, Rabbi Simon Sherman reluctantly married his daughter, Fanny and "The Goya", George Washington Eaton.

When my sister, Helen, was born, the Sherman family was ecstatic:
"What a beautiful baby!"
I was born almost three years later and everyone in both families, the uncles, the aunts and the cousins were overjoyed:
"A boy and a girl, you have a perfect family!"
Less than three years after I came into this world, twins, Simon and Betsy, were born. A lot of clucking and murmurs simmered through the Eaton family and a collective, "Oy, Vai iz mir," through the Sherman family.

By the time the fifth child, little William, was born, all the Jewish, as well as Gentile relatives, threw up their hands in frustration.

In spite of the depression, my father held his radio technician position at RCA's Camden, NJ plant. The Depression's effect on RCA's business deteriorated to the point that George and the plant's chief and RCA founder were the only employees left in the RCA plant. When the chief asked his only remaining employee, George, to sweep the floors, the proud technician refused a task he deemed too demeaning and was fired on the spot. Leaving RCA, my father opened a radio repair shop. His radio repair business could have been successful, but too often he left his shop to look at real estate with Aunt Leona's husband, my Uncle Will, and the radio repair business ultimately failed.

My mother often lamented, "Customers wouldn't get their radios repaired as soon as your father promised, and they never knew when the shop was open, because your father was off gallivanting with your uncle to look at properties."

Another local man that had a radio repair shop in the same years my father had his shop. Unlike my father, this repairman kept regular shop hours and later became a highly successful electronics and appliance merchant in Philadelphia. Whenever his advertisements appeared in the newspaper or on television, it served to rub salt in my mother's wounds, and she could only grit her teeth and dream of what might have been.

The Great Depression dragged on and my parents were forced to move from their beautiful home in Philadelphia's Mayfair section to renting an old row home in South Philadelphia. Fired from RCA, a failed radio repair business, and the scarcity of work during the Great Depression were setbacks that my father faced in providing for a wife and, at that time, two children, Helen and me. He managed to scrape up odd jobs as an electrician in a shipyard and a steel mill, work that was often dangerous. Another one of my father's painting shows him changing light bulbs in the rafters of a steel mill, high above the blast furnaces. Obviously it was a perilous job, but he had to risk his life to put food on the table for his growing family.

After four extremely, lean, hard years, with the birth of the twins making it a family of six mouths to feed, my father landed the city's radio technician job in West Philadelphia. On my fourth birthday, our family moved to a new life of opportunity on 44th Street.

CHAPTER SEVEN
FAMILY DINNERS

Our family's dinner table was the designated time that the entire family was expected to convene to eat and review the day's activities. We discussed everything and anything. Often conversations became lectures on the importance of doing well in school and ultimately the achievement of a college education.

I could see by the way my father fidgeted in his chair that he was still agitated over his tussle with Mickey and Ricky. Finally, the head of the house decided to shake off his aggravation and got down to family business,

"When does your school start?"

"School starts on Monday," Betsy volunteered.

Mom interjected, "You know we can't afford a college education for all of you, but it's imperative that all of you are going to college. This means you must do your best to get excellent grades -you know that?"

"Yes Mom," we chorused.

My biggest fear was realized when my mother turned her attention to me, "Geordie, you and your brothers were gone most of the day. What did you boys do today?"

Lowering my head into my dinner plate, I mumbled, "Si and I delivered our newspaper routes and later we just fooled around with Don and Bob at Sam's."

"Geordie, please don't mumble! I heard the newspaper part, but the rest was lost to my ear."

Noticing sounds of muffled giggles coming from my two brothers, Mom turned to them and asked, "What are you two snickering about?"

Before answering their mother, Si and Billy peeked over to see my threatening laser-like glare. If looks could kill, my brothers were dead, and their smiles disappeared as if a cold and wet washcloth had swept across their faces.

Si squirmed and sputtered, "Nothing Mom . . . really."

"William?"

"I just thought of something funny. Now, I don't think it was so funny."

Leaning across the table and wagging her finger at the three of us, my mother began another lecture in Yiddish, which she usually followed with the English translation:

"I don't like secrets. *Dray zakhn ken men nisht bahaltn; libe husn im dales.* As they say in Yiddish, there are three things you can't hide: love, a cough, and poverty. Are you three hiding one of those or something else?"

Our mother was a linguist; proficient in Latin and well versed in French, German, and Yiddish. She mostly enjoyed using colorful Yiddish expressions to emphasize a point and delighted in their clever, literal translations. A nervous sweat began to pour from every pore in my body. I had to think of something quick before one of my brothers would collapse under the pressure of my mother's wagging finger spiced by Yiddish and spill the beans on our stupid caper. Aha! Why didn't I think of it sooner? A sure-fire way to change the subject suddenly occurred to me.

"Hey! Helen, are you ready for school?"

My older sister was an excellent student, but she constantly worried over her studies. Invariably, she'd come home crying, "I flunked that test! I know I flunked!" Later, when the grade was reported, she not only passed, she had received another "A" or "A Plus."

I couldn't have planned it better, because Helen launched into her patented litany of fears and complaints, "Mom, I'm sure that school is going to be too difficult this year. I'm taking Solid Geometry, Calculus and German."

In an attempt to placate her daughter, suspicions toward her sons were dispelled, and Mom's attention was diverted to her eldest daughter.

"Now, now, don't worry Helen. Your father can help you with your math and I'll be able to tutor you in German."

My sister's concerns weren't mollified by these assurances. "Golly Mom. You know I'll need a scholarship to go to college, but I'm sure my grades won't be good enough."

Helen's persistence evoked another Yiddish saying: "Mein Got, Helen, you work so hard and you always get A's. There's another old, but fitting Yiddish saying: When someone complains and there's nothing to complain about: 'Kaleh iz tsu sharn.' Literally, the bride is too pretty. Now, please eat your dinner and quit your worrying."

"Hah! Fanny, that's a good one! I hadn't heard that one before."

"Thank you dear. How about tonight? Will this be a late job?"

"I'm afraid so, because Victor Borge's show at Convention Hall is bound to run late, and I'm going to have to leave soon to set up the sound system. I'm going to enjoy the show, because Borge's such a great entertainer and his brother, George, is the nicest guy you'd ever want to meet. He's a real gentleman."

We had been so drilled by our parents that all five of us would have a college education, but considering our family's financial situation, Understandably Helen felt that her only chance for college was to achieve top grades and earn a merit scholarship. I felt a pang of guilt in instigating my sister's concern for her grades at school. I may have taken advantage of my sister's concerns, but I had to do it to keep my brothers from cracking. My brothers and I exchanged knowing glances and smiled - the subject had been officially changed.

Mother continued to preach to us, "You all must do well in school and study as hard as your sister Helen, if you expect to go to college, *and* all of you *are* going."

49

College was a constant theme in the household. Despite limited finances, each one of us understood that a college education was expected, and somehow we'd make it happen.

"Yes Mom, we know, but what if we don't get scholarships?" Helen asked.

"You have to have faith that somehow the Lord will provide, and that's that."

Evoking the lord to placate Helen wasn't evidence of my mother's religious leanings, but was more a reflection of an innate optimism. Even though our mother favored her own Jewish religion, she rarely exhibited strong religious beliefs and didn't take an active role to guide us to her Jewish faith, but ironically would still be concerned if anyone of us appeared to lean toward the Christian faith.

"Oh . . . George, what happened with those hooligans? You were so upset I thought it would be better to ask you when you cooled down."

"Geordie said the two punks were Mickey and his buddy Ricky. They must've thrown a rock or something at the front window. I gave the two of them a good shaking."

"A rock! Oy, vai iz mir! Those awful hooligans! Let this be a lesson to all of you. Stay away from that crowd, they're no good!"

We chorused again, "Yes Mom, we know."

Giving up on her complaints about school, Helen offered a bit of neighborhood news.

"I heard that Weird Wally took off again. I saw the police at his house again this morning."

Wally lived with his parents in a first floor apartment, directly across the street. Wally was not exactly all there. In fact, he spent most of his time not being here. He came by his nickname, "Weird Wally," due to his penchant to take off to parts unknown. He was a tall, spectacled, blond teenager, and he always seemed to be plotting his next escape. He had a certain strange look in his eyes that was a bit too scary for us guys. Even though Weird Wally was my age, he hardly ever joined our neighborhood group's games. We didn't complain–we felt safer without Wally.

Fortunately for the neighborhood Wally wasn't psychotic – his only known neurosis was wanderlust. After hours or days of search, police would eventually return Wally to his parents from the Thirtieth Street railroad station, a bus depot, or somewhere as far away as Chicago. Where did he get the money to take off? No one knew – it was a mystery. Did his parents really want Wally to be found? No one could say for sure.

It was Simon's turn to speak, "Mom, can Buddy's mother really talk to the dead?"

"For heaven's sakes what in the world gave you that idea?"

"That's what everyone's saying. Since Buddy died, they say she can talk to dead people through Buddy. Didn't you see the line of people outside their house today?"

"Kain einoreh!" Mom sighed, "I imagine parents that can't rub two dimes together and dress their children in shmattehs are desperate. They'll do and say almost anything. Anyone that believes that someone can converse with spirits must be as meshugeh as she is. It's all a lot of superstitious mumbo jumbo - don't you believe it."

"Yes Mom!"

My siblings and I enjoyed the daily lectures at the dinner table that made each meal informative and provocative for us. Our "Yes Mom" responses were respectful, but there was a touch of fun involved. Not to be left out in the news department, Betsy jumped in with a bit of news of her own:

"I talked to Jimmy Bumstead today. He said he's got a new uncle." My parents exchanged knowing glances and winked.

Jimmy Bumstead was a nice, skinny, little, eight-year-old, with a squeaky voice, who lived with his mother in a first floor apartment at the Locust Street corner.

During the war, Jimmy's father was off fighting the Nazis and freezing his ass off during the Battle of the Bulge while his wife entertained servicemen in her first floor apartment. Jimmy's mother made her living in supporting the war effort by lifting the morale of a parade of servicemen. The new faces that entered their home were introduced to little Jimmy as his "uncles." In the evening, a lamp in the window, covered with a sheer, red veil, was like a homing beacon for the lonesome sailor or soldier.

When victory over Japan, VJ Day was announced and World War II had ended, the weary warrior, Jimmy's father, returned home from the wars to his wife and son. The war veteran found his wife in bed with one of the "Uncles." Instead of being the least bit embarrassed or apologetic at her husband's discovery, Jimmy's mother chased the returning veteran-husband out onto the street and threw his belongings after him. After the eviction incident, the "neighborhood" believed that Jimmy was traumatized in seeing his mother oust his real father from his life. Sadly, the only family he could relate to was the Dagwood Bumstead's comic strip's family, a happy and normal family life he could only wish for.

Squirming in his seat, and anxious to add something to the table's news, Billy couldn't restrain himself any longer, "Hey! Now, it's my turn!"

All attention turned to the youngest son, waiting to hear what he had to say. I coughed loudly and glared again at my little brother. Alert mother's eyes darted from Billy to me and back to Billy. Just as he glanced to see daggers fired from my eyes, tiny beads of sweat began to appear on my little brother's forehead. The skylight incident and the jump might have been a great story to tell at the dinner table, but Billy realized that the consequences might outweigh the value of the tale that he was dying to tell.

Billy stammered, "Oh, never mind. It's not important. Uh . . . what's for dessert, Mom?"

Even though her motherly antennas were still quivering with suspicion, she was diverted by little William's question and proudly announced:

"Since you all did such a good job in eating your vegetables, I have a special dessert for you–Lokshen Kugel."

The dinner ended with a flourish of voracious Lokshen Kugel eaters. Mom might not have been as good a cook as her Jewish sister, our Tante Leah and her sister-in-law Aunt Mary (Not tante for some reason), but our mother's cakes, pies and puddings were undeniably the best.

Si, savoring the delicious noodle dessert, asked, "Mom, [mmmph] may I have another helping?" .

"Not now. Your eyes are bigger than your stomach, your mouth is still full, and you haven't even finished the Kugel on your plate."

She may have admonished her son, but it warmed her heart to hear how much her children liked her Kugel. When plates were licked clean, the children were excused from the table. Mom and Pop sat alone at the dinner table to discuss matters that they'd prefer that their children not hear.

"George, how'd you do on the civil service exam?"

"I received the top grade, but that doesn't mean a damn. Another guy has the inside track for the promotion."

"How can that be? If you do so well in the exam . . . we can barely make ends meet now."

"I know. I know. When it comes to city jobs – it's all politics. The civil service exams are a sham. When it comes down to it, the best test results don't trump who-you-know. God Fannie, you know I'm working as much overtime as I can get"

"All the more reason that I wish you'd be more civil with my sister. I don't know what we'd do without her rent money."

Before my aunt and uncle had moved to our third floor apartment, Tante Hinda often loaned her younger sister money to help our family survive from one modest city paycheck to the next. When Uncle Nathan was forced to retire from his cutter's

53

trade, my mother reciprocated her sister's earlier generosity by renting the third floor apartment to her sister and husband. Unfortunately, this became a source of friction in our household. Inexplicably, Pop resented the in-laws' intrusion in his home, even though the apartment was available and was designed to generate much needed rental income. There were occasional flare-ups of resentment by Pop, and Mom was repeatedly forced to defend her sister and husband's right to live on the third floor.

Pop slid angrily back in his chair saying, "Geez, Fannie, don't let's get into that. I gotta get going to work."

Pop stomped out of the kitchen, leaving a distraught wife in his wake. Long after my father departed for his work at Convention Hall, the Rabbi's daughter remained in her chair, head bowed, elbows rested on the table, and hands enveloping her face. She began to sob. The stress of raising five children on the meager income of a city radio technician was almost too much to bear for this highly educated, intelligent woman. Born into a well-off Rabbi's family, my mother had known a much more comfortable life.

Seeing Pop leave, I hesitated at the kitchen door and looked in to see Mom in tears at the kitchen table and overheard her lament: "We . . . can't make ends meet."

Scarcity of money remained an issue in our home. Before I could earn my own money, I recall the time my mother couldn't afford me a dime to go to the movies with my friends. As a little kid I wasn't able to understand, and I remember how much I cried from disappointment. Another remembrance of the lean years was when my father had been forced to prepare a dinner of celery soup, because celery and milk was the only food in the house, and my mother had gone to bed crying from sheer frustration.

In witnessing my mother alone in tears at the dinner table, I then realized the toll that financial struggles had taken on her.

CHAPTER EIGHT
MY HOME IS MY CASTLE

The morning following my misguide leap, I was in the kitchen hurriedly drying the breakfast dishes and immersed in thoughts of yesterday's events and in anticipation of another planned two-hand-touch football game on Locust Street. On the one hand I was afraid that the police might appear anytime at the front door and arrest me for breaking the skylight and still plagued with regret that I didn't leave the porch to help Pop deal with the crumb-bums, Mickey and Ricky.

I was looking forward to the football game against the tailor's son and his Armenian buddies. They were older than us guys and we'd probably get beaten as usual, but they were a lot of fun and I loved football.

Just as I began to turn my thoughts to the crazy leap from the garage roof that had seemed to make some kind of an impression on my friends, the doorbell rang.

RIIING!!! The sound of the front doorbell brought me back to earth. Could it be the police?

From the living room, I heard Mom call out, "I'll get the door Geordie."

No one else was at home. My brothers had gone ahead to the deli to join our friends for the football game, while I finished doing the dishes. Helen and Betsy were visiting their girlfriends, and Pop was at work.

When Mom opened the front door, she was shocked to be met by an angry mob that had overflowed onto the porch and spread down the front steps. Confronting her were two large, brawny, and angry looking men, Mickey and Ricky's fathers. Among the crowd behind the fathers were their sons, some of the notorious

Ludlow Gang members, and even that pain-in-the-ass, Peck. They all appeared angry and growled like a lynch mob. Rope, rail, feathers and a cauldron of hot tar were the only things missing in that crowd of ugly faces.

With the mob growling support behind him, Mickey's father stepped up to confront my mother. He snarled, "Where's your husband lady?"

"Who are you and what are you all doing here on my porch?"

"I'm Mickey's dad, and this here's Ricky's dad. Now, where's your husband?

"He's not here."

"Don't give me that shit! He's probably hiding in there!"

"What in the world do you want with my husband?"

"He roughed up our boys and we're here to kick the shit out of him!"

Again, the crowd roared in support.

At that, Fannie Sherman Eaton straightened out her 5'4" frame, thrust out her ample bosom and pronounced, "I'm sure your sons deserved exactly what they got. Now, get off my porch this instant!"

"Like hell we will!" The mob chorused.

Ricky's father, a man astonishingly more ugly than his son, poked his face inches from my mother and hissed.

"If you say your husband's not home, where's Geordie? If your husband can beat up my son, I guess I can give the same to his boy."

"GO AWAY FROM HERE! He's not home! All of you . . . get off my porch immediately!"

Listening to all this through the open front door, I remained out of sight in the kitchen. I was certain that it wouldn't be healthy to reveal myself to that angry crowd.

"BULL SHIT!! We're comin' in and see if they're in there!"

Now, this rude exclamation really got Mom's English dander up. Hackles rose from her reddening neck. The little woman seemed to grow a full foot in height and her bosom swelled with pent up anger. In an even more defiant voice, the former

56

Suffragette, London born, college educated woman measured every word with her cultured English accent, that sounded every bit as regal and powerful as Britain's Queen Mary.

"MY HOME . . . IS MY . . . CASTLE! Leave my porch *immediately*, or I'll call the police and have the lot of you arrested for trespassing!"

My mother's defiance flustered the angry fathers and her loud proclamation caused the two men to stumble back a step. Instantly, it was as if a wet blanket had been thrown over the mob's belligerence. They were stunned by this little woman's declaration of resistance. The perplexed mob leaders looked at each other, hesitated for a moment, shrugged their shoulders, and sputtered something unintelligible to each other. Finally, the two fathers turned and slowly led the grumbling crowd off the porch. The disappointed and frustrated lynch mob continued to grumble curses as they shuffled away down the sidewalk, a far cry from the gang that had come for blood.

I could hardly believe my mother's courage in the face of that angry crowd. It didn't take long before admiration of my mother led to feelings of guilt for not standing by my mother's side. Why didn't I help Mom? Just as I was beginning to feel a little better about my stupid jump from the garage roof my psyche was being washed away again with self-incriminations, concerning my failure to confront the mob and assist Pop against Ricky and Mickey.

Hearing the front door close, I sheepishly shuffled out of the kitchen to meet my brave mother. Like all sons, I loved my mother, but the manner in which she stood up to that irate crowd cast her in a new light, a heroine's light. Her courage put me to shame.

Unable to look her in the eye, "Mom, I'm sorry that I didn't face that gang with you."

"Don't be Bubelah. They were a mean spirited bunch, you did the right thing, and you know what they say, "Discretion is the better part of valor,' and my dear I assure you that discretion was called for in this situation."

"Gee, Mom, you were great the way you ran those guys off!"

"Thanks for your praise, but let that be a lesson for you. I meant it when I said my home is my castle."

RIIING !! My embarrassment was spared, when I heard the phone ring in the dining room, and I ran to pick it up.

"Hello, Eatons!"

"Is that you Geordie?"

I immediately recognized the voice of my Aunt Sadie, Pop's oldest sister.

"Yes, Aunt Sadie."

My widowed aunt, Sarah Eaton Phillips, lived alone in a little bungalow, off of Tabernacle Road, back in the pinewoods of Medford Lakes, New Jersey. Like my father's other sister, Leona Eaton Dickhart, our Aunt Sadie was a tall, handsome, large boned woman. Her two children, Buddy (Paul) and Jean had their own families and lived in Medford Lakes not far from Aunt Sadie's home.

When I was ten years old, our family made its first visit to see the Medford Lakes property before Aunt Sadie finalized her purchase. We toured the acre property that was surrounded by Pine trees and met the nice, aged colored couple that was selling the property to our aunt. Our aunt's purchase was a bit too rustic for us city folks, because the only thing that approached indoor plumbing was a water pump at the kitchen sink. A foul smelling outhouse was nestled in the pinewoods' perimeter. From the very beginning, the outhouse was repugnant to my citified family, but "when ya gotta go, ya gotta go."

While everyone was gathered in the kitchen, I continued my investigation of the house and discovered a shotgun standing in the living room's corner. A shotgun was a new and curious thing for me, and I decided to pick it up to show the family   Entering the living room, I waved the shotgun, which happened to be loaded, and shouted, "Hey everyone–look at this gun, will ya!"

To my amazement everyone ducked for cover, except Pop, who shouted and strode toward me, "Don't touch that trigger and point that gun down-NOW!"

I didn't know what all the fuss was about and couldn't understand why everyone was crouched on the floor. As soon as my father rescued the gun from my grasp, my family and the old colored couple emitted a loud sigh of relief that sounded a lot like steam escaping from a locomotive at West Philadelphia's 30th Street Station.

Even though nerves were rattled from the gun incident, all was forgotten when the pleasant, old colored woman served up a freshly baked and the most delicious, huckleberry pie. It was the first huckleberry pie I had ever eaten, but it would not be the last.

In the ensuing summers, we discovered that huckleberries were plentiful along the pinewood paths, which made visits to Aunt Sadie fun and delicious. Pop would take the five of us kids on hikes through the wooded paths and we picked huckleberries for Mom's pies. Pop would caution us, "Now, listen to me carefully children. Don't pick the larger berries from the taller bushes. Those are inkberries – they'll make you sick and give you writers' cramp. Pick only the smaller berries from those lower bushes."

As directed, we passed up the tall blueberry bushes, which seemed to be the same berries we bent over to pick, but they were larger. We listened to our father's caution and dutifully bent down to collect the smaller huckleberries off the lower bushes. On more than one occasion, I happened to look back to catch Pop eating berries from the tall shrubs. This was just one example of our father's unique sense of humor in tricking his offspring to bend down to pick smaller berries while he could stand and enjoy eating larger berries from the taller bushes. I'd chuckle to myself, but I never ratted on my father to my brothers and sisters. In a way, I got a kick out of my father's weird sense of humor, which he was often wont to employ.

"Is your father home?" Aunt Sadie asked.

"No Aunt Sadie. He's at work."

"Then . . . let . . . me . . . speak . . . to . . . your mother."

Because my aunt uttered each word so emphatically, I sensed she meant business. Aunt Sadie was more of a disciplinarian than an affectionate aunt to us kids, unlike our Jewish aunts. My father's Christian sisters, Leona and Sadie had married earlier, raised their children to be married and have children of their own, and seemed to merely tolerate my siblings and me, but their children were nice to us, even though they were considerably older.

This was in contrast to the welcome and affection we enjoyed from our Jewish uncles, aunts, and cousins. Our Jewish relatives lived in neat row homes in predominantly ewish neighborhoods, and the moment we entered their comfortable homes our nostrils would always be filled with delicious aromas of our Jewish aunts' cooking for the holidays. They were fabulous cooks and our cousins were congenial and loads of fun. On holiday visits, dinners began with kefilte fish served with red horseradish, matzoh, a tiny glass of Manischevitz Port wine, and followed by chicken soup with a tasty matzoh ball. A brisket or chicken with tzimmes (a dish of sweet potatoes, carrots, and chicken fat) was normally the next delicious course, and the meal ended with a fantastic lukshen kugel that would be the coup de grace to a great meal. If our Jewish relatives weren't celebrating a holiday together, there would be a joyful wedding or bar mitzvah as an excuse for more exquisite food.

But my most significant recollection of Aunt Sadie was her shouting, "Shut the screen door!" Actually, it was an understandable demand, because New Jersey Pine Flies were the worst pests imaginable. In our walks through the woods, the wretched Pine flies would harass you for miles, biting at bare flesh and trying to eat you alive.

"Mom, Aunt Sadie wants to speak with you, and she sounds angry."

It was only two weeks earlier that the entire family had vacationed at Aunt Sadie's house, while she took her T Model Ford on a long road trip with a friend. Putting the phone to her ear, my mother began to speak in the sweetest and cheeriest tones.

"Hello, Sadie. When did you get back?"

Her sister-in-law's voice trembled in saying, "I got home last night. Fanny, I thought I was doing your family a real favor, staying in my house for a week."

Taken aback by Sadie's words and angry tone, Mom was instantly puzzled.

"Certainly Sadie, it was most kind of you."

"My house has needed painting for some time, and paint is peeling on the weather side. You know don't you, that your husband promised to paint my house while I was away?"

"Did he say that?" I didn't realize that he made that promise – I'll have to talk to him." The sister-in-law remained curious at the tenseness in Sadie's voice.

"Yes . . . he did! Do you know what he *did* do?"

"No, I really don't."

Aunt Sadie sputtered and sounded as if she could hardly restrain herself.

"Your husband, my brother, left me with an oil painting of my house . . . An OIL PAINTING! Can you *believe it*?"

With what little spare time he had, Pop had recently taken up oil painting. He had taken his painting paraphernalia along to his sister's house to do a little dabbling while he was on vacation. Before departing on her trip, Aunt Sadie had asked Pop to paint her house as compensation for the family's stay in her home. He may have agreed to his sister's request, but he had no intention of spending his much needed rest and relaxation by painting his sister's bungalow. After our aunt's departure, Pop resolved that he deserved a real vacation despite his sister's demand.

61

Instead of laboriously painting Aunt Sadie's home's exterior, I can only imagine that he impishly conjured up the idea to do an artistic rendering of his sister's cottage. Certainly, my father must have realized his sister wouldn't appreciate his attempt at humor, but he couldn't resist the temptation to play one of his little jokes on her. This was just another example of our father's quirky sense of humor that was enjoyed by many, but could be a source of exasperation for others. Unfortunately, on this occasion, his sister was one of the exasperated. In truth, Aunt Sadie rarely enjoyed her "little brother's" humor.

Mom's initial reaction to the news was annoyance with her husband, but a second thought of the matter prompted her to place a hand over her mouth to stifle a giggle. Managing to control herself, she launched into an expression of sympathy:

"Oh my, that's not right, Sadie! You have every right to be angry with George. I'll speak with him as soon as he gets home. I had no idea what he'd promised you. I saw him doing a little painting, but he wouldn't tell me what he was painting. Let me assure you that George will call you as soon as he gets home. You were *so* kind to allow us the use of your home and what an *awful* way for him to repay you."

As soon as Mom hung up the phone, she was torn by exasperation with Pop's silly prank, but found it impossible to suppress a smile.

"What's so funny, Mom?"

"Your father, that's who. Now, go out and play and forget what happened with that crowd."

I left the house, headed for the deli, to join my brothers and friends. Hustling down the street toward the Locust street corner, I heard the sound of a mocking voice close behind.

"Ha, ha, ha, my home is my *castle*."

I'd know that voice anywhere–it was Peck. I turned and met Peck's sarcastic, smiling face. He was dressed as sloppy as ever. His hand-me-down pants were two sizes too large, torn and dirty.

His tee shirt was riddled with holes and stained even worse than his pants and teeth.

"My home is my castle," Peck sneered, again mocking my mother's declaration to the mob.

Instantly, an unusual and overwhelming feeling of rage swept over me. Except for minor scuffles with my brothers, I had never fought anyone. But Peck's smirk and his ridiculing my mother ignited in me an extraordinary and fierce reaction. In a sudden bull rush, I knocked Peck flat on his back onto the pavement and sat down hard on his chest. Peck couldn't have been more surprised at my reaction to his taunt than I was. Angered at myself for not facing the mob with my mother and fueled by my anger at Peck's disrespect to her was too much to bear and I took it all out on Peck.

"OWW! Whatcha doin'!? Geordie, get the hell off me!"

"You'd better say you're sorry, or I'm gonna punch you in the nose."

"I hit my head - let me up!" Peck whimpered.

"You made fun of my Mother, and you'd better say you're sorry."

"Okay, okay, I'm *sorry* . . . you're hurtin' me," he whined. "Now, let me up."

"Say, *please*."

"Okay, *please*."

"Say, pretty please."

"Dammit! Pretty *please!*"

As I stood up and allowed Peck to go free, I felt a warm glow of satisfaction. How great it was that I won my first fight, and I put that pain-in-the-ass Peck in his place.

"Now, get out of here Peck, and watch what you say from now on. Next time, I'll beat your brains out – that's if you got any!"

Without a word, still whimpering and rubbing the back of his head, Peck limped back up the street toward his home. In retreat, he glanced back at me and I could see the bewilderment in his eyes. The look that Peck gave me almost erased the guilt I harbored from hiding in the kitchen and hanging back on the porch while my parents fought the good fight.

With renewed confidence I raced to the Deli for the football game.

CHAPTER NINE
STREET FOOTBALL

By the time I got to Sam's deli, the two-hand-touch football game had already been organized, and play was about to begin. The Armenian tailor's son, whose father owned the shop next to Sam's, and his visiting Armenian buddies had challenged our guys to another game. It would be a tough game, since the Armenians were at least three or more years older than any of us and had easily beat us every time. Even so we liked to play them, because they were a happy and friendly bunch. They made losing the game almost a pleasant ritual. Besides the age difference, the Armenians had a unique advantage - they didn't need to huddle. At the line of scrimmage, in their native tongue, the quarterback would call plays aloud to his team, and direct the receivers as they were running their routes. The Armenians knew what they were doing, but we didn't have a clue.

It wasn't easy playing a game of touch football in the middle of Locust Street – there were plenty of obstacles. Our so-called "football field" had a fairly steep grade from 44th to 43rd Street. Parked automobiles on the curbed sidelines narrowed the playing field, and moving vehicles caused delays and were even hazardous at times. A football game was frequently delayed by passing automobile and truck traffic, cars and delivery trucks going in and out of the Acme market's parking lot, and truck deliveries at Sam's. Goal lines were the deli at one end and the fire hydrant in front of the Philadelphia Evening Bulletin's Branch Office at the other. Si and I were carriers for the Bulletin and delivered newspapers from the Locust Street's branch office that was commanded by its captain, Wolfie, who was infamous as the Neighborhood Nazi, but that's another story yet to be told.

I was happy to see that Harry had joined our team. He had good hands for a receiver and we were sure going to need him. Since Harry was an Irish Catholic, he went to Sunday Mass with the younger Ludlow Gang members, but he didn't flaunt his relationship with them like the hated Peck was prone to do. Harry's curly red hair and freckled Irish face was matched by an overly confident, wise-guy air, but to his credit-in a friendly way.

"Hi, Geordie," Harry greeted me in our huddle. "I heard about your jump off the roof. That was something."

"Oh yeah, it's no big deal."

It was encouraging that some guys might think I did something big, but I worried that the garage's management or the police might learn about my exploit as fast as Harry had.

"Geordie, they won the toss, and we gotta kick off," Don announced.

"Okay Don, thanks."

The two teams lined up at either end of the street's "field." In the street game of touch football, because of the narrow and short dimensions the practice was to pass the ball on the kickoff instead of kicking. I passed the ball as hard as I could from the fire hydrant goal line. The kickoff-pass was caught by Sammy, the tailor's son, at the deli's goal-line, and he began to run down the street's hill behind a wall of his blockers. Our team ran up the street's slope, tried to avoid blockers, and attempted to tag the runner. I was able to dodge between two of the blockers and I planted two hands on the runner's hips. There ensued the usual two-hand-touch argument:

"I didn't feel two hands – I only felt one."

"Baloney, I got you with both hands!"

Sammy laughed it off - he was that confident they would win, "All right Geordie, I'll let you have this one."

I laughed right back, "Don't do me any favors – you know I tagged you!"

Smiling, Sammy shouted to his team something in Armenian, which might have been a wisecrack, but I hoped it was, "Line-up!"

The tailor's son was the lone player in the backfield, and four of his teammates were in a straight line at the line of scrimmage. There was a lot of laughter and conversation going on among the Armenians, but we couldn't understand a word. Gadget was our designated "rusher," but touch football's rules dictated that he could only walk in unless the ball was fumbled, he was blocked, there was more than one player in the backfield, or the ball carrier would begin to run forward. If the lone rusher stood on the scrimmage line and counted to ten, then he was permitted to run in and attempt to tag the ball carrier or passer with two hands. Those were the general rules of two-hand-touch football in the West Philadelphia streets, or at least they were our rules.

On first down, after the quarterback shouted instructions in Armenian to his team, the ball was centered underhand to the lone back, Sammy. He threw a nice pass in the general direction of a wide-open receiver, but the pass was slightly overthrown and the football bounced off a parked, blue Buick. The quarterback received a lot of friendly derision from his teammates, in Armenian of course.

On second down, Sammy again overthrew his receiver badly and the ball bounced off the windshield of a parked Chevrolet sedan. I didn't have to understand Armenian to know that the tailor's son was subjected to another dose of friendly abuse. Even though his teammates were only teasing him, the quarterback was rattled.

On third down, I read the quarterback's eyes and stepped in front of the receiver to intercept the pass. On the run back, I dodged the hands of two would-be tacklers/taggers and almost scored a touchdown, but I was tagged a car-length short of the deli's goal line.

My teammates were ecstatic, "Way to go, Geordie!"

In our offensive huddle, acting as quarterback, I whispered the play to the team:

"Alright now, Harry, lineup on the left and cut over in front of that blue convertible. Si and Don . . . you criss-cross in front of the deli, Bob . . . buttonhook at the yellow car. Gadget . . . center to me on two."

"Why can't I go out for a pass?" Gadget whined.

Si hissed, "Aww . . . shut up Gadget!"

I said, "Listen, if we don't score now, we may never get another chance."

Gadget wasn't satisfied and stomped his foot in protest, "It's not fair!"

"We're letting you play and that's plenty fair."

In spite of his protest, Gadget scuffed his way over to the ball, and centered it back to me. I was surprised to see my receivers execute their designated routes - they rarely followed the plays called. Bob was covered in front of the yellow auto, Don and Si collided on their criss-cross maneuver. Si fell to the street, in pain from running into Don's elbow. Don stopped dead in his tracks to put a hand up to touch his bloody nose.

The confusion caused by Don and Si's collision distracted the Armenian defenders and Harry broke free past the deli goal-line to stop in front of the blue convertible. I couldn't get a good grip on the football, because the ball's inner bladder was coming through the laces and made the ball oversized. Luckily, I managed to partially spiral, partially shot-put a pass on the money into Harry's hands for a touchdown. Our guys could hardly believe it, since we never had a lead and hardly ever scored against the Armenians. In all the games we had played with them, you could count on one hand the number of times we had scored a touchdown. It was a cause for jubilation.

The Armenians were as amused at our celebration as they were surprised by our touchdown. We came down to earth, when they reestablished their dominance and scored three successive touchdowns. I made a few good run backs on kickoffs and played well on defense, but we didn't come close to scoring again. The slaughter ended when the tailor came out of his shop and called to his son to assist him with an alteration. The football game was officially called on account of inseam measurements.

Walking back to the deli's steps, Harry put a hand on my shoulder to stop me.

"Geordie, I've played touch with you enough to know that you're a damn good football player. Touch football is okay, but I've been playing tackle football with some of the guys from Ludlow Street. If you'd like to play, I think I can get you into a game."

Si overheard Harry and his face turned beet-red.

"Tackle football and with *the Ludlow Gang* would be NUTS!?"

I looked at Si with disbelief. I couldn't understand why my brother was so upset.

"Relax Si. I didn't say I'd play. Harry, I dunno. Maybe I'll play – I just don't know. I've never played tackle football and I don't have any football gear, pads, shoes, helmet - nothing."

"Are you kidding? No one has helmets or anything. Anyway, when there's a game, I'll letcha know. Seeya guys." Harry took off for home.

Thinking about Harry's tackle football suggestion, I recalled last year's Philadelphia Eagles game at Shibe Park. On a bitter, cold day in November, I shivered through an Eagles game against the New York Giants. The Eagles team had some terrific players: NFL's star running back Steve Van Buren, Tommy Thompson, the one-eyed quarterback; Pete Pihos, a terrific, glue fingered tight end; and Wild Man Willy, wild and crazy, but a great defensive end. Even then, I was intrigued with the idea of playing tackle football. If my parents would let me, I thought it might not be too horrible to play with the Irish Catholics from Ludlow Street. How bad could it be? I'd soon find out.

Even though we lost the football game to the Armenians, we regrouped again on the deli's steps. I described the mob's invasion at our house, Mom's valor, and my conquest over the pain-in-the-ass Peck.

"Boy! Am I glad you put down that bum, Peck. He's been asking for it for a long time!" Si accented his words by pounding his fist into his palm.

"Thanks. I don't think he'll be such a smart-ass anymore."

"Do you think that mob will be back? Don asked.

"I don't know about the mob, but Ricky and Mickey sure won't give up."

Billy jumped up and announced, "Wow! I almost forgot. My buddy, Porgie said he'd be here this afternoon with a bomb that he built."

We all gasped, "A bomb?"

"Yeah, that's what he said."

Porgie was Billy's friend and classmate at Henry C. Lee elementary school. Porgie's hobby and claim to neighborhood fame or infamy was making small bombs. He had access to lots of chemicals from his father's pharmacy stock. Porgie's father owned a number of pharmacies in the Philadelphia area, which gave his son unlimited access to chemicals that he used to create small cap-like bombs. His form of neighborhood entertainment was to place these small bombs on the trolley tracks and wait for the next trolley's passage. When the trolley's wheels hit the cap, a tiny explosion would cause the wheels to bounce up. The result was some startled trolley passengers and really pissed off motormen.

"When's he gonna be here? I asked.

"He didn't exactly say."

"Look who's coming," Dave whispered to the group. "It's Jane and Tootsie."

Jane lived with her parents in an apartment over the tailor shop. Jane was a year younger than me, but extremely well endowed for her age . . . or any age. Jane had a pretty freckled face. She and her parents had moved to West Philly from Dubois, PA. Her up-

70

state Pennsylvania twang made my Philadelphia accent sound almost Shakespearean. But as a person, Jane was as genuine as pure gold.

Tootsie was a pretty, dark-haired daughter of a popular radio evangelist in Philadelphia. As full figured as Jane was, Tootsie was as thin as a rail. A while ago Jane had told me in confidence that Tootsie had a crush on me, but I could only consider Tootsie as a friend. In fact, the relationship of boys and girls in our neighborhood was free of sexual tension. We had grown up together and were good friends-more like brothers and sisters. However, this didn't prevent my buddies and me from admiring Jane's ample breasts, alluringly protruding beneath her white, cotton blouse. As much as we were intrigued by Jane's mature figure, not one of us had the maturity or a clue on what to do about it.

"What are you guys doin' today?" Jane asked.

"We just finished playing some football and we're waiting for Porgie to show up with his bomb," Billy chortled.

Tootsie's dark eyes opened wide, "Bomb? You said bomb?"

I smiled, "Yeah . . . he said bomb."

"Huh! Well then . . . I guess we'll stick around."

Tootsie deliberately sat down beside me. While we waited on the deli steps for Porgie and his bomb to appear, we chatted and laughed. Crowds of football fans began to walk by us down Locust Street on their way to Franklin Field and Penn's opening football game against the University of Virginia. I could hear about a mile away the faint strains of Penn's Red and Blue Marching Band playing the Quakers' fight song, *Red and Blue*, as it marched down Spruce Street and into Franklin Field.

Bob whispered, "Hey, did you guys see that gorgeous blond with the red and blue blouse?"

"You bet I did! She was [wheeze] a real dish – that's for sure," Don said, taking a long laborious breath and dabbing at blood still oozing from his nose.

Almost every home game at Franklin Field filled the stadium with 75,000 cheering fans. Penn played competitively against some of the best college football teams and players in the country.

Contrarily over at Shibe Park, 21st and Lehigh Avenue, the professional football Eagles were not so fortunate. The Eagles drew a mere 28,000 for their 1948 National Football League championship against the Chicago Cardinals. In those years, University of Pennsylvania's football was *the* game in town for Philadelphia's football fans.

My appetite to play tackle football was aroused in this heavily charged football atmosphere: Penn's football fans, dressed in the school's red and blue colors, streaming down Locust Street with pretty co-eds wearing large Chrysanthemum corsages, all smiling and laughing on their way to the game, while sounds of Penn's band serenaded the scene.

I mused aloud, "Someday, if I got good enough, maybe I could play at Franklin Field."

Billy's eyes suddenly lit up. He jumped to his feet and shouted, "I see him! Porgie's coming!"

CHAPTER TEN
THE BOMB

Even from a distance, it was easy to recognize Porgie in his way of wobbling, not walking, down Locust Street hill. Porgie was a short, chubby kid with tight, curly, blond hair. When the jolly bomb maker arrived at the Deli steps, Don noticed a cardboard shoebox under Porgie's arm.

"Whatcha got in that box? Don asked.

"The . . . *bomb*," Porgie said with a broad, evil grin.

Our admiring group echoed with hushed, almost reverent tones.

"The . . . *bomb*."

We knew, if Porgie said it was a bomb, it had to be a real bomb.

"Where's it safe to set it off, Porgie?" Si asked.

"The jolly bomb maker chuckled diabolically.

"Safe? Who said anything about safe?"

I pointed across the street and said, "How 'bout the corner lot?"

Many years ago a house on the corner had burned to the ground, and the lot had remained vacant, covered with weeds and bricks. It was the safest place I could think of and of little use, but for a bomb. An alleyway separated the lot from the Acme market, which should have been a reasonably safe distance from the bomb site's ground zero.

Porgie attempted a poor imitation of a mad scientist in the latest horror movie.

"Ah yes – the lot should do nicely. Hee–hee-hee."

"To the lot!" Bob shouted.

Our group chorused.

"TO THE LOT!"

In crossing the street, and all the way into the lot, we chanted:

73

"The bomb . . . the bomb . . . the bomb . . . ."

Porgie halted in the middle of the lot and held up his hand for attention. With a flourish, the roly-poly bomb maker slowly eased a Campbell's Tomato Soup can from the shoebox, a fuse dangled from one end of the can. "Oohs and Aahs" arose from his admiring and curious audience. Everyone moved in and formed a tight circle around Porgie as he carefully placed the can onto the ground.

"When I light this fuse, you'd better stand back. I made a new mixture of chemicals so I don't know exactly the bomb's power."

Absolute, rapt silence descended over us as we watched the fuse sizzle brightly and the sparkling twine advance inside the can's mouth. We waited with bated breath . . . waited . . . and waited. There was a long moment of suspense. Nothing appeared to be happening. All eyes turned to Porgie with puzzlement, then doubt, and for the moment even disgust reared its ugly head.

Billy's curiosity consumed him and he bounced forward to peek inside the can.

"It probably went out." Billy announced his conclusion as he bent over to peer inside the can.

Not knowing whether or not the bomb was going to go off, but I sensed that my brother could be in danger, I rushed forward and shouted.

"Get the hell back!"

I yanked my brother off his feet and pulled him back just as the bomb went off.

KABOOM!!!

The bomb's eruption was an ear splitting, ground trembling, window-rattling, smoke billowing event of momentous proportions. The explosion scared the wits out of the amorous couple that had been necking in a blue sedan parked on the curb adjacent to the lot. In the bomb's wake, the sedan roared away from the curb, tires squealing, approaching NASCAR speeds on its escape's track down Locust Street.

Initially, Porgie's face had the look of Doctor Frankenstein, who has just witnessed his monster's first breath. The rest of us

74

could only express shock from the startling explosion, and instinctively fell back and away from the blast. We couldn't believe what just had happened and stood riveted in place for several moments. Finally, the enormity of the eruption's sound and the clouds of smoke that billowed up and spread over us caused panic.

Breaking my brief paralysis, I shouted.

"JEEZ! LET'S GET THE HELL OUTTA HERE!"

Imitating a startled herd of rampaging Texas steers, I led the race off the lot onto Forty-Fourth Street. I had no idea where to run, but I only knew we had to make a whole lot of distance between the lot and us. At the sound of the blast, startled neighbors had rushed out of their houses onto porches and out onto the pavements. Jimmy Bumstead's mother, still in her nightgown, peeked out her front door. I galloped in the lead and glanced across the street at my house to see our nice, next-door neighbors standing agape on their porch.

"WHAT HAPPENED?" The old couple shouted.

I ignored them and kept running like a maniac, but what worried me the most was a glimpse of my mother in the living room's window. When she recognized her own offspring running like frightened deer, ahead of clouds of smoke swirling up from the corner behind them, she abruptly yanked down the window's shade. "Oh, oh, I'm going to get it, when I get home," but escape from the scene of the crime seemed to be far more pressing at the moment.

We continued our flight and I maintained a growing lead over the panicky crowd behind me. After covering three blocks on a dead run, I pulled up in an alleyway and hunkered down behind a wall. One by one the others reached my hiding place. To our collective horror, sounds of sirens and bells filled the air and seemed to be coming from every direction. Fire trucks and police cars streaked past our alleyway hideout and roared down the street toward the lot.

"*Jesus*, [wheeze] [pant] we're in real trouble now," Don gasped.

75

Bob hollered, pointing an accusing finger at the little bomber, "What in the *hell* did you have in that bomb, Porg?"

Porgie's earlier flamboyance and cockiness had been replaced by fear, and he was drenched in sweat.

"Stuff," he blubbered.

"What do you mean STUFF?" Bob screamed.

In between sobs, Porgie replied, "I don't [sob] remember exactly. Some different chemicals and stuff that usually works good and only more of it and anything else I could [sob] get my hands on that seemed good."

I walked up to Porgie and slapped my hand onto his shoulder.

"Porgie,this better be the last time you bring your damn bombs into this neighborhood. We're all in a hell of a lot of trouble, if the police find out. I know my brothers and I are gonna get it, when we get home."

We stayed hidden in the alleyway's refuge for an hour or more. When we hadn't seen a fire truck or a police car pass for quite a while and sounds of sirens were no longer heard, I came to the conclusion that it might be safe for all of us to head home.

"I think the coast is clear," I said. "Let's get the hell outta here, go home, and face the music." Bob got to his feet, gave Porgie a shove, looked out up and down the street, and walked out of the alley. Porgie appeared to be on the verge of crying again, but gathered enough courage to slink home. Jane and Tootsie were afraid to move from their hiding place, but they knew they had to leave the alley sometime, and they crept together out onto the pavement. Don, my two brothers and I slowly walked back toward our respective homes.

The second my brothers and I entered the front door, we heard Mom calling from the kitchen.

"Boys, is that you?"

Jeff greeted us in the hallway with excited howls and leaps, his brown and white tail wagging like mad. He delivered plenty of licks all around.

"Yeah Mom, we're home," we responded together.

"Come into the kitchen. Your father and I want to talk to you."

Jeff didn't understand the seriousness of the situation and happily trotted with us on our fateful procession down the hallway that could have been accompanied by a funeral dirge, *Dum-Dum-Dee-Dum-Dum*. Whatever our punishment would be I hoped it would be quick and not too painful.

Before entering the kitchen I listened carefully to be certain I didn't hear the sound of gallows being constructed. The three of us walked slowly into the kitchen with our heads almost reaching the floor. I dared not look my parents in the face, and my brothers were similarly cowed. When I risked lifting my eyes from the floor, I cringed at the sight of my parents seated at the kitchen table, arms crossed, with looks that could melt steel.

"What in *hell* caused that explosion?" Pop demanded.

"It's all Porgie's fault," cried Billy.

"We had no idea that it would do that," Si said.

"Yeah, Si's right. We had no idea that Porgie could build a bomb with that much power," I muttered.

Pop waved his hand in disgust, "If the police come to get you three, they can have you. I hope they lock you all up and throw away the key."

Mom added, waving her hand in disgust, "You boys must be meshugeh to let that Porgie explode bombs across the street from our home, or anywhere for that matter. Your father came right from work, when I called him. Kain einoreh! It's a miracle no one was killed."

"Pop, I'm really sorry – we didn't know," I said.

"Sorry and didn't know is not good enough . . . son. We'll have to see what comes of this."

That was it, the gallows weren't built and we were spared swats with a belt. The fear of consequences had not passed, and we'd have to wait and see what the morrow would bring.

CHAPTER ELEVEN
THE NEIGHBORHOOD NAZI

The day following "The B*omb*," Si and I rode our red Schwinn bicycles down to the Bulletin's Branch office on Locust Street, several doors down from the Deli.

My brother and I delivered newspapers for the Philadelphia Evening Bulletin seven days a week. The Bulletin's Branch office was nothing more than an empty storeroom with splintery dark wooden floors. The room was dimly lit by two low wattage light bulbs dangling from an open, black ceiling. The only furnishings were two well-worn, wooden benches against the wall on the right side of the room. The Branch Captain's small office was partitioned off in the far left corner.

When we entered the room, a large stack of thick Sunday newspapers was piled in the middle of the room. The wire strapping around the bundles of newspapers were unbroken, so we realized that we were the first carriers to arrive, but we didn't see Wolfie, the branch captain.

Wolfie, a senior in high school, was an imposing and fearful figure to all the newsboys. He always wore blue jeans and a tight fitting black tee shirt that highlighted the curves of his muscular build. His jet black hair was closely cropped and the highly polished black boots completed the Hessian persona that he admired so much. Wolfie was known as the "Neighborhood Nazi." He had earned the moniker by fancying himself as the famous Nazi Panzer commander. Even in the midst of World War II, Wolfie idolized Field Marshal Rommel, the Nazi's Panzer commander. His adoration began with Rommel's victories in the North African campaign, but it didn't seem to matter to Wolfie that the Nazis and Rommel were our country's mortal enemies. One of Wolfie's favorite tactics to intimidate us was his simulation of Panzer attacks that began with a bull-rush and ended with a newsboy flat on his back on the hard wooden floor. The Nazi would finish off his victim with a cleated boot pressed down on the newsboy's chest until he heard a painful squeal.

"Another victory for Rommel over those dirty, Limey bastards!"

Wolfie delighted in ruling the Branch office like a Stalag commandant and terrorized the newsboys.

"Hey Geordie, where do you think Wolfie is?

"Shhh . . . keep it down, Si. The door's open, so he must be in his office," I whispered.

Wolfie must have heard us, because the tyrannical leader stomped out of his office.

"You two little jerks are late!"

My brother and I shivered a little as Wolfie strode toward us with his boots making a loud clomping noise with every step. The oncoming, scowling juggernaut should have frightened Si speechless, but he summoned the courage to croak a response:

"But . . . But . . . But . . . Nobody else has gotten here."

No one dared to render any form of dispute toward Wolfie, but Si had, and the reaction was predictable.

"WHAT DID YOU SAY, PUNK!? THE HELL WITH EVERYBODY ELSE! I'M TALKING TO YOU! I oughta kick your little asses outta here! You're ten damn minutes late! Now, you two little bastards get your papers and your asses moving outta my sight!"

Wolfie counted out our allotment of papers, shoved them in our faces. After stuffing the papers in our canvas bags, he practically booted my brother and me out the door. For fear of feeling Wolfie's boots' steel tipped toes, Si and I leaped over the two steps to the pavement. Wolfie glared at us from the doorway as we hung our bags over our bikes' handlebars.

Wolfie loomed from the branch's doorway and shouted, "ACHTUNG!! You're too damned slow . . . I should've kicked your asses! GO! GO! GO!"

Mounting our bikes, Si and I pedaled away as fast as we could, still fearing Wolfie's boots and still feeling his icy glare. We didn't stop pedaling until we were safely out of the Nazi's sight across 43rd Street. We dismounted and leaned our bicycles against the Divinity school's fence.

"Let's see what the newspaper says about the bomb," I said.

"Yeah, I sure hope nobody squealed on us."

"Don't worry, Si. The police would have been at the door by now, if they knew it was us."

I pulled one newspaper from my bag and began to leaf through the pages until I came to a surprising heading, ***Strikers Bomb Market.***

I read the article aloud to Si:

"Late Saturday afternoon, the police and fire department investigated an explosion at an Acme market at 43rd and Locust Streets. Police suspect that disgruntled Acme strikers had set off a bomb on the roof of the market, where bomb material was discovered by investigators. The extent of damages to the building has not been determined. A getaway car, a late model blue sedan, was sighted leaving the scene after the explosion. There have been no arrests and no named suspects, but police promise a thorough investigation and arrests."

How could the newspaper's account be so wrong? Several things contributed to the distortion of the real story: A shift in the wind had caused the smoke from the explosion to cloud over the Acme market. Coincidentally, the Acme workers were in the midst of a workers' strike. The so-called "bomb making material" discovered on the market's roof by the police was nothing more than a soup can and some wires that Harry had tossed up there several weeks earlier.

The couple seen necking in the blue sedan, who were engaged in an afternoon tryst were too embarrassed or confused to come forward to incriminate us. Most likely, they were too occupied in their lovemaking and too frightened by the explosion to know what really happened. When I finished reading the newspaper article, I looked at Si and took several deep breaths of relief.

"Boy, did they get the story wrong," I laughed. "Wait until Mom and Dad read this story. Maybe they won't be so hard on us, but I wouldn't bet on it. We'd better get going. If the Nazi should come out of the Branch and see us here, he'll plaster us."

"You don't think he'd really come this far to get us, do you?" Si chuckled.

"I wouldn't bet on that either," I shouted back as I rode off to begin delivering my newspapers.

I delivered 150 newspapers every day except Sunday's delivery wasn't quite as big. My delivery route covered about six city blocks. My deliveries included row homes, apartment buildings, and a convalescent home. There could be serious delays in deliveries at the convalescent home, since my very old and lonely customers tried their best to draw me into long conversations. Even though I had gotten to know and grown to like my aged customers, there were a lot of papers to deliver, and I was anxious to get on to complete my route. Most often, I'd be relieved to find the old souls napping,

My last stop was on 42nd Street at a house where Philadelphia's meanest Cocker Spaniel lived. I hated that dog and the Spaniel definitely hated me. The dog's owner did her best to keep the black monster from getting at me, but one day, the snarling beast escaped from the house and bit my right index finger. In one way, I hated the dog because of that attack, but his bite turned out to be an unexpected stroke of luck.

My father escorted me to the nearby Osteopathic hospital's emergency room to be treated. The attending doctor must have been more familiar with repairing broken bones than dog bites, because after the doctor stitched my finger's wound, he applied a splint to my finger that was almost large enough to support a broken arm. He capped off his oversized work by wrapping the splinted finger with a ton of gauze.

The next day, I had an appointment with Mrs. Schwartz for my weekly piano lesson. I hated piano lessons, but my parents wanted all their children to learn to play the piano. As I approached the piano teacher's home on Buckingham Place, I wasn't my normally reluctant, piano student self. There was a spring in my step as I bounced up to the piano teacher's front door and rang the doorbell.

"Oh, hello Geordie, it's about time you got here little late for your lesson."

"I'm sorry Mrs. Schwartz, but you see." I held out to her my heavily bandaged and splinted finger.

My piano teacher reacted as I had expected, "My lord! What in the world happened to you?"

"I'm sorry Mrs. Schwartz. I'm not going to be able to take my piano lesson today – a dog bit my finger."

"My, my, that's too bad.

Actually, Mrs. Schwartz feigned concern. She was quite aware of my limitations in music and severe lack of piano playing talent and desire. My sister Helen and little brother Billy showed much greater promise as piano students, and the piano teacher had realized almost immediately that she was wasting her skills trying to make a pianist out of me. In a week or so the wound healed and the splint and bandages were removed. By that time, my parents had accepted the end to my piano career. Thus, the combined efforts of the vicious Spaniel and the overly zealous Osteopathic doctor did everyone a favor.

I was relieved to make my last delivery for the day, but I looked anxiously over the fence that separated the meanest Spaniel's home from the home of pretty, dark haired, teenage, twin girls. I lusted after the pretty twins like only a teenage boy can do. The twins went to a parochial school, which limited my chances to meet them. During school months, I would do my utmost to time the day's final delivery to coincide with the twins' return from school in their neatly pressed, white blouses and Kelly green uniforms. I pretended not to stare at them and they did a pretty good job of ignoring me. I was too shy to speak to the twins, so it was unlikely that I would ever meet them, but fate would eventually make the impossible possible.

After completing my deliveries, I returned home with our family's Sunday newspaper under my arm where I found my parents sitting in the living room. Pop was in his chair and perusing Helen's Calculus textbook. Only he could enjoy reading a Calculus text, but that was the kind of guy he was. Mom was sitting on the sofa leafing through the *Ladies Home Journal.*

"Hi Pop. Hi Mom."

"Hi Sunshine."

"Good morning Bubelah. Is that the Sunday paper you have there?"

"Yes it is! " I smiled contentedly and handed the newspaper to Mom and flopped down beside her. Jeff appeared from nowhere and jumped onto the sofa and squeezed between Mom and me. The Beagle pawed at my arm, demanding to be petted. To keep Jeff happy, I began stroking his long, velvety, brown and black ears.

"Here Mom, read the article on page nine."

Mom slowly leafed through the newspaper's pages until she came to the bomb article and read it aloud for Pop's benefit. When she was finished reading, Mom carefully placed the newspaper onto her lap.

Anxious to know what she thought I asked, "Well?"

My mother glanced at her husband and turned to look me in the eye. Her brow furrowed and an "oh, oh" shaped my lips. I thought she'd be pleased to read that my brothers and I were free of suspicion. She might have even thought that the article was funny, but the stern look she gave me was unexpected, which caused me to fidget and giggle nervously

"Hee-hee-hee. They got it all wrong. Isn't that funny?"

Mom wagged a finger in my face.

83

"Got zol ophitn, God forbid that you should regret what happened. It's nothing to laugh about. You're very lucky that no one was killed or seriously injured and none of our neighbors told the police what really happened."

"Your mother's right, it tain't funny Magee," quoted by my father from the Fibber Magee and Molly radio show.

"Oh dear!"

"What's the matter now, Fannie?"

"I just remembered. Your sister, Sadie called yesterday."

"Did you tell her how much we appreciated the stay at her place?"

"Of course, I did."

"What did she say?"

"If your sister spoke Yiddish, she would say to you, A gezunt in dein pupik."

"What? For crying out loud-what do you mean by that?"

"It means, thanks for nothing, or in literal terms–thanks in your belly button."

"Why? What kind of reaction is that?"

"Why? You have to ask why? You promised to paint her house and you only gave her your oil painting of her house-that's why. She's mad as hell."

Pop stared back at Mom with a completely blank look. Then, an impish smile began to appear then widen on his broad face, followed by a sputtering sound and said, "I guess my sister didn't like my painting."

As much as Mom tried to suppress her smile, she couldn't contain herself. Suddenly both of my parents were consumed by the silliness of the joke that Pop had played on his poor sister, and the two burst into laughter.

Relieved that the bomb interrogation was over, I thought it was pretty funny too and laughed along with my parents.

CHAPTER TWELVE
TACKLE FOOTBALL

We could hardly wait to see how Flash Gordon would escape from last week's impossible and death threatening predicament. At the Commodore's Saturday matinee, I, Don, Bob, Si, Dave, and of course, Gadget, sat in our usual place in the theatre's fifth row. But true to form Flash Gordon once more escaped from what was last week's inescapable trap. It was a certainty by the end of today's episode the hero would find himself in another death threatening predicament. Just as Flash Gordon fired his ray gun at the evil Emperor Ming, the screen blackened as four huge men shuffled in the row in front of us and sat down. It didn't matter that they sat, because they were so big we still couldn't see the screen.

I whispered, "Golly, that's Steve Van Buren and that's gotta be some of the Eagles."

"Geez, they're big," Bob said.

Steve Van Buren was the Eagles star running back was the team's first draft pick from LSU in 1944. In the 40s, star professional football running backs didn't earn a multi-million dollar salary, and they didn't live in mansions on Philadelphia's exclusive Main Line. Because Van Buren's starting salary was a mere $4,000, the prized rookie and football star lived in a modest apartment in our neighborhood.

My interest in playing real football was aroused by my football hero's appearance in front of me, Harry's suggestion that I play tackle football with those Ludlow Street guys, street football was beginning to feel too tame to me, and the sight of happy Penn's football fans streaming toward Franklin Field. Steve Van Buren sitting in front of me in the Commodore theatre must have been an omen that I couldn't ignore.

After the movie, the guys and I returned to the deli's steps to formulate our plans for the rest of the day. Si went into the deli to get a Coke, and we began to discuss how Flash Gordon might escape sure death in next week's episode.

"He really got himself into a pickle this week. I don't think he's got a chance," Billy said.

"Don't worry Gadget. He'll escape – he always does," I said.

Don turned his head to spot Harry running toward us at full tilt.

"Why's Harry running?" Don announced. "He's sure in one hell of a hurry."

Harry pulled up panting in front of the deli's steps, and gasped, "Geordie, jeez [pant] . . . boy am I glad I found you. We've got a game of tackle football . . . [pant] at the Catholic Church . . . over on Chestnut Street . . . in fifteen minutes. I told the guys about you [gasp] . . . and we need another player."

Si came out from the deli and heard enough of Harry's urging, and his face reddened like it always did when he got agitated.
He howled, "Geordie, you can't play with that Ludlow Gang! If they don't kill you, Mom will!"

Don nodded, "Don't you remember that Mickey and Ricky wanted to beat you up just last week?"

"I wouldn't do it, if I was you," Bob said, shaking his head.

Billy squeaked, "I'm gonna tell!"

Harry stamped his foot and shouted, "Clam up you guys! Geordie can make up his own damn mind!"

In spite of the chorus of warnings from my brothers and friends, the desire to play tackle football had reached a bursting point in me, and this could be my first shot at playing some real football.

"Okay, I'll play, let's go, Harry."

"Terrific! C'mon we gotta hustle."

"You guys better not say anything to Mom or Pop . . . or else."

Harry and I took off on a fast trot, while a cacophony of warnings and threats continued behind us.

"YOU'LL BE SORRRRREEEEE!"

About a block from the church, I began to have second thoughts. For the very first time, I was about to meet the fearsome, infamous Ludlow Street Gang. Maybe, my brothers and friends were right, and I really would be sorry.

I stopped in front of the church. "Harry, wait a sec. I'm not too sure about this."

"Gee, Geordie. Don't worry. They're really good guys."

Reluctantly, we kept going and I followed Harry onto the Catholic Church's lawn. Ahead of us, I spotted six guys at the edge of the church's well groomed, grassy lawn that bordered one side of the church. The group abruptly halted their conversation and turned to eye Harry and me as we approached.

Harry shouted, "Hey, this is Geordie, the guy I told ya about!"

My uneasiness was increased by the curious, up and down looks I was getting. What was I, an animal in the zoo? At least they all looked pretty normal to me: about my age, two eyes – set apart, two arms – not overly long, two legs – fairly straight, and no tattoos or visible facial scars.

The largest in the group strutted up to me and extended an enormous hand.

"I'm John."

John was a tall, blond guy, with a muscular build that he had developed from helping his older brother, Butch deliver kegs of beers to the local taprooms.

"So . . . you're the Jew boy that Harry's been talking about. Do you think you can play tackle football?"

Being called a Jew boy confirmed my fear in coming to play with the Irish Catholics. My Methodist father and Jewish mother offered more than enough confusion at home. Except for my Jewish aunts, uncles and cousins, most Jews considered me a *Goya*. To add to the dilemma, except for my close friends, most Gentiles considered me a Jew. Our parents had married, despite family objections, gave birth to five children, but never resolved their religious differences. My siblings and I were left with no religious foundation to call our own.

87

On the few Sundays I had gone to the Methodist church on 45th Street with Don and his parents, my Jewish mother would give me the silent treatment, and my Methodist father would give me an "Atta boy!" Contrarily, when Tante Hinda took us kids to the synagogue on Jewish holidays, we would return home to a brooding father. As a result, we couldn't satisfy either parent, when it came to religion,

Because of the parental conflict over religion, our home was virtually devoid of worship of any faith. Christmas was celebrated with a decorated Christmas tree purchased on Christmas Eve. At that hour, the Christmas tree's price was right, but the quality of the tree was wrong. Trees purchased on Christmas Eve often required Pop to drill holes in the tree's trunk and move branches around to cover bare spots. Baby Jesus wasn't mentioned as part of our Christmas celebration. My siblings and I believed in Santa until someone let the cat out of the bag that there was no Santa, but Christmas presents still appeared under the Christmas tree and gifts were exchanged.

The high Jewish holidays; Passover, Rosh Hashanah and Yom Kippur; were celebrated at dinners in the homes of our Jewish aunts. Pop gladly accepted these Jewish holiday observances at homes of Mom's sisters, because he thoroughly enjoyed Jewish food and the Jewish women were terrific cooks.

I decided to ignore John's "Jew" greeting. I thinly smiled at the big guy, and shook his hand.

"Yeah, I think I can play tackle football."

"Ya think so, huh. Well, we'll soon find out. See here. Take a look at these boots."

John pointed down to his heavy, leather, army boots. If I were to guess at the size, I'd have to estimate they were size humungous.

"I see 'em."

"Well, if you try to tackle me with these boots, you're gonna get a mouth full of leather."

Harry pleaded, "Geez take it easy on him, will ya John. We wanted him to play, right?"

One by one, the others stepped up and introduced themselves. There was Smitty, tall, thin, and dark haired; Rinny, blond and a little chubby; Charlie, jet black hair, medium build and very muscular; and identical twin brothers, Jack and Wally. They didn't look that much different to me than my own pals. I faced a group of tough Irish-American kids that would be as docile as altar boys at Sunday's Mass.

Because this would be my first game of tackle, and I'd be playing with guys that my friends and I had feared for years, my butterflies felt like bats flapping in my stomach. Except for Harry, none of these guys seemed ready to accept me as a fellow football player. I was beginning to seriously regret agreeing to play, but I knew it would be too embarrassing to leave. I repeated to myself: Hang in there Geordie, you're about to play tackle football on a grassy field, instead of touch football on the Locust Street hill.

Sides were quickly chosen. Harry, the twins and I formed one team and John captained a team of Charlie, Smitty, and Rinny. Jack held the ball upright with one finger and Harry kicked the ball down the field. Grabbing the ball on one hop, John began to lumber straight up the field. Lumbering was the best way to describe John's running style. He was slow and the boots made him slower. John seemed to think he was invincible and dared anyone to tackle him. Judging by my teammates who exhibited half-hearted efforts to tackle John, they appeared to be more afraid of tasting his boots than trying to tackle him.

On Harry's kick, I ran downfield as fast as I could to intercept the ball carrier, but Charlie blind-sided me with a strong block that knocked me to my knees. John ran by me and laughed to see me on the ground. It was bad enough to be blocked like that, but to be laughed at made me determined to get up and go after John. I jumped to my feet and gave chase. My speed and John's heavy boots allowed me to overtake him. With a dive, I plowed my shoulders into the backs of the runner's legs.

Shocked, the ball carrier hollered.

"WHAT THE . . . !"

His long body lurched forward and he plummeted like a fallen tree.

THUD!

"WHAT THE HELL! WHO . . . WHA . . . HIT ME?"

John struggled to roll over and get up. He saw that I still had a grip on one leg.

"Me."

"YOU!"

"Yep – it's me," I said with a self-satisfying smile.

John got to his feet. A slight grin crept across his lips and blossomed into a full-blown smile.

"That was quite a tackle for a Jew boy."

"Isn't that what I was supposed to do?"

"Yeah – it sure was, but I'll be damned, I didn't think you had it in ya. Sure ya never played tackle before?"

"I'm sure."

I looked around at the smiling faces of the guys that, only minutes ago, had given me a cool reception. This one tackle had broken the ice. Now, they seemed to be more like regular guys, nothing like the Ludlow Gang that I had dreaded. When play resumed, I showed my quickness in running down ball carriers and my ability to make good open field tackles. With each tackle, John and the other players exchanged knowing glances. On fourth down, I dropped back to bat down John's pass to Charlie over the middle.

Now, it was my turn to show my stuff running with the ball. Our team huddled.

Harry encouraged me, "Keep it up Geordie, you're doing great."

By now my nervousness had disappeared and I was anxious to carry the ball. It was good to know that a mere tag with two hands couldn't stop me – it would take a solid tackle. Taking the center snap, I took off and galloped around right end. It wasn't just better than average speed that made me a good running back. My elusiveness gave me the ability to make quick fakes and moves that were developed from two-hand-touch football on a narrow city street. I ran for a touchdown on my very first carry as player after player barely touched me while I zig-zagged my way to the goal line. They hadn't seen running like that, and it was encouraging to hear their compliments.

"Boy, you're a helluva runner! Where didya learn run like that?" John asked.

"I play touch football almost every day, and ya gotta have moves."

On my next opportunity to carry the ball, I scored another touchdown, but this time I had broken through John's outstretched arms and leaped over Charlie's diving tackle attempt. My self-confidence soared with every run on offense and every tackle on defense. The game was a new and exhilarating experience for me, but it all came to a crashing halt, when a large church door opened and a robed priest appeared.

"John, I'm sorry, but you and your friends should know that you aren't permitted to play on church grounds. Please go, or I'll be forced to call the police."

Showing deference to the priest, John called back.

"Okay father, we're leaving right now."

I was disappointed – I was having a great time. We all shuffled grudgingly off the church grounds and gathered on the pavement in front of the church. Being chased from a game wasn't a new experience for me, and I was sure that the Ludlow guys had plenty of the same disappointments. About to head home, I noticed that Harry and John were bunched together with the other guys and engaged in an animated conversation. Before I could leave, Harry called:

"Hey. . . Geordie! Wait a minute!"

John, Harry and the rest of the group trotted up to me.

John asked, "How would you like to play on our football team? We've got a bunch of guys together to form a team, and we're gonna play other neighborhood teams."

"You gotta do it Geordie! We need you," Harry said.

"Gee, I don't know. I'm not sure if my parents will let me."

John towered over me, "Ask 'em. We're gonna have a meeting at the corner of 43rd and Walnut Street next Saturday at one-o'clock. We can really use you."

Harry stepped in, "We already have a team name – the 49ers!"

John looked annoyingly at Harry.

"Yeah, that's what I was gonna say. Our team will be the 49ers and it'll be a hell of a lotta fun."

Feeling good about the impression that I had made, but convincing my parents wouldn't be easy. "I . . . I'll really try." I gave a parting wave and walked home, deep in thought. How was I going to tell my parents? Was there even a chance that they'd let me play with the Ludlow guys? It was a lot to think about.

CHAPTER THIRTEEN
FOOTBALL DEFENSIVE

Upon arrival at home and still excited over my first tackle football experience, I entered the house to catch a succulent aroma emanating from the kitchen that made me realize I was famished. A roasted leg of lamb in a bed of roasted potatoes and caramelized onions was one of my mother's finest culinary accomplishments. My appetite was certainly driven by the exhilaration created from the football game and the energy expended. I felt that I could consume the entire leg of lamb without any assistance. When I walked into the living room, I looked for my brothers, but they weren't home yet.

Mom's voice came from the kitchen.

"Who's there?"

"It's me, Mom."

"Geordie? Dinner will be ready in an hour. Where are your brothers?"

"I wasn't with them. I think they're at Sam's."

Seeing one of my favorite books, *The Three Musketeers,* on the table by the window, I picked the book up, fell back onto the sofa and began to read. It wasn't long before my brothers noisily entered the house and spotted me in the living room. Si and Billy slowly approached, examining me from head to toe, expecting to see evidence of horrible, life threatening injuries. There were none. They were sure that I would come home bruised and bloodied and seemed to be disappointed that I wasn't damaged. Except, for a few grass stains, there was no evidence their brother had played tackle football with those mean Ludlow guys.

"Are you Okay?" Si asked.

"Yeah, I'm fine."

Billy whispered, "Did you like playing with them?"

"It was fun and I played really well."

"Did they play dirty?" Si asked.

"Nope, they're actually pretty good guys. They tried to scare me at first, but I showed them I could tackle and run with the ball. I scored a couple of touchdowns before we were chased."

We abruptly changed our conversation as soon as we heard Pop at the front door. When Pop entered the living room, he looked exhausted. Pop looked beat most of the time, but he hadn't lost his fatherly intuition that told him we were hiding something.

"Hi, boys. What're you up to?"

Trying to conceal the guilt in my voice, I mumbled, "Uh, nothing. We were just talking about something."

We heard Mom's voice from the kitchen, "Is that you George?"

"Yeah, it's me, Fan."

"Dinner will be ready in two hours."

"That's fine. I'm gonna take a little nap."

Pop gave the three of us a quizzical look. He wasn't convinced that nothing was up, but fatigue overcame him and he slumped into his chair. I could see that he was too tired to speak or even open one of his favorite radio magazines. The moment he sank into his chair, his second bed, Pop's eyes closed, and his loud snoring began seconds later.

My brothers went up to their room to await Mom's call to dinner. A little later, Helen and Betsy strolled in and were greeted by the family's Beagle, who had just been let in from the backyard.

Our backyard was small, but my parents had made it into their prized garden by planting varieties of flowers in almost every square inch of soil. Pop fertilized their prized garden with vegetable peelings and coffee grounds. My parents particularly loved roses and their various colors and varieties were featured throughout the garden. A narrow path led to a concrete slab bench with brick leg supports that my versatile father had constructed.

With the pressure of raising five children and limited financial resources, caring for the garden was much needed therapy for my parents. They loved flowers and the garden was their treasure.

Before dinner time Pop had gotten up from his nap and went down to his workshop in the cellar, and Mom called out to me from the kitchen..

"Geordie, go down to the cellar and tell your father to come up for dinner."

"Okay Mom."

The door to the cellar was just inside the kitchen's entrance, and the steps leading down to the cellar were steep and dimly lit. A coal furnace sat in the middle of the cellar's concrete floor, and the coal bin was up at the far end near the street. Because of the poor lighting, unfinished concrete walls and furnace fumes, the cellar was the last place I wanted to spend time, but this is where Pop spent much of his waking hours at home.

I found my father in his usual position on a stool by the workbench. His eyes squinted in the dim light of a single incandescent light bulb hanging above his head, and a damp cigarette dangled from his lips. It looked like he was trying to solder something to something.

"Oh Geordie, I didn't hear you come down. C'mon over here Sunshine . . . I want to show you how to solder this wire onto the crystal radio I'm making."

It would be about the hundredth time my father would try to teach me to solder. In fact he tried to teach me a lot of things that I wasn't interested in.

"Pop, Mom sent me down to tell you dinner's ready."

"Oh, okay, I'll be right up."

When Mom served dinner, the table conversations began promptly.

"What did you do today, Helen?" Mom asked.

"I studied math with Mildred."

Mom beamed. That's what the matriarch wanted to hear.

"Good."

That's what the father wanted to hear.

"Very good," Pop said with a broad smile.

95

"And you . . . Betsy?" Mom asked.
"I helped Helga decorate her bedroom."

Helga's parents owned a wonderful German bakery. When Helga visited, she would often bring loads of delicious pastries. I liked the Apple Strudel a lot, but I enjoyed seeing Helga even more. Helga was a very pretty, athletic, dark haired girl, who roller skated competitively. I never thought I'd have a chance with Helga, and I was too shy to tell her I liked her. My shyness with girls of interest started from the time I declared my affection to a tall, pretty, redhead in 5th Grade. I was spurned by six simple words, "You're too short for me," a rebuke that scarred my young, male ego. The redhead moved to Indiana before my growth spurt caught up with hers.

Young men, where were you all day?" The mother continued her queries.
"We went to the movies and fooled around with the guys afterwards." Si and Billy replied in unison.
"And Geordie weren't you with your brothers?"
"I went to the movies with them to the movies, but I played football later with some other guys."
"What guys?" Pop's interest was piqued.
Slumping in my chair, I mumbled softly. "Harry and some others,"
Mom didn't like Harry, who she thought was a "toughie," and was almost afraid to ask about the "others."
"Others, who are these *others*?"
Billy couldn't resist the temptation. He was bursting to drop the bombshell and exploded with the news:
"They're the Ludlow Gang – that's *who*!"
"Oy, vai iz mir! Gang, what do you mean gang?" Mom gasped as she held her bosom, feigning a heart attack.
My idiot brother forced me to speak up, "They're not bad guys. They want me to play on their football team, and I really want to play tackle football."

"Tackle football! Mein Got! YOU'LL BREAK A LEG!"

To my surprise, Pop said, "Hold on, Fannie. You know, football might do Geordie some good. He's big enough and old enough to play in a team sport."

Tears came to her eyes as Mom wailed, "*Hob rakhones!* Have mercy on me George–our son will be hurt playing with those ruffians."

"Now, now, Fannie, I promise you . . . I'll watch over Geordie and the team."

Using her apron as a handkerchief, Mom began to wipe her tears away and leaned toward Pop, glaring directly into his eyes. In measured tones, my Queen Mary Mother made a chilling pronouncement.

"All right, George! I wash my hands of this and it will be on your head, if he gets hurt."

The remainder of the dinner continued in absolute silence. Everyone buried their heads in their plates and the usual family conversation was suspended. I wasn't happy with the rift that developed between my parents, but I was elated to realize that I had been given, albeit reluctant, approval to play tackle football. I enjoyed every bite of my dinner. Until this time, my father and I had infrequent one-on-one sessions. He tried to teach me things like mixing cement for the front and back steps, changing washers in faucets, changing the car's water pump, or soldering radio wires.

Lack of interest in my father's attempts to be more adept with tools was a disappointment for him, because he believed that all these handyman skills should be passed down from father to son. In Pop's era, a man needed to be able to take a car apart and put it back together, repair a household's electrical and plumbing problems, and do a myriad of other things.

My father believed in tough love and rarely displayed overt affection, but I still felt he loved me. Emblazoned in my memory is the time I encountered my father on the second floor's landing.

Unexpectedly, he gave me a painful swat across my behind, and I whined, "Ow! What was *that* for?"

"That was for nothing, just in case you might do something," he said and laughed.

But, for the first time to my surprise, Pop had come to my defense in something that really mattered to me–playing tackle football, and I couldn't be more grateful.

CHAPTER FOURTEEN
THE 49ers

All the way up 43rd Street headed toward my first meeting with the 49ers, I was afraid that I might be entering the lion's den. Misgivings and negative thoughts ran amok in my head: "Hell, I don't know these guys, Mom doesn't want me to play with them, and I might not be good enough." As much as I wanted to play tackle football, I paused at least a dozen times, and I almost turned back on half of those hesitations.

Overcoming my fears, I rounded the corner onto Walnut Street and came upon a large group of noisy teenagers. At first, they ignored me. They kept on laughing, talking loudly, and playfully pushing and sparring with each other-just horsing around. I recognized some of them as the guys I had played with last week on the church grounds. My eyes continued to scan the group until I spotted Harry talking to big John at the far edge of the crowd. Just as I recognized John, I caught his eye, and the big blonde's face lit into a huge grin.

John shouted, "He's here! Hey Geordie c'mon over here!" Conversations ceased and all heads turned in my direction. I was ten minutes late for the meeting, and John and Harry were relieved to see me. John was afraid that his newly discovered football player wasn't going to show, and he quickly elbowed his way through the crowd.

"Guys, this is the Jew boy I was telling you about. He's a great tackler," John stopped to laugh and pounded me on my shoulder. "I should know – Hah - and a helluva running back."

Looking around at all the strange guys staring at me, I thought that maybe they had never seen a Jew before. I might have mentioned the fact that I was only half Jewish, but figured that it wouldn't make much difference to them.

Harry added, "I played touch and tackle football with Geordie, and I swear he can run really great."

John raised both his arms above his head and shouted to make his voice heard above the noise from Walnut Street's bus, truck and auto traffic streaming out of center city, headed for the western suburbs.

"Listen up you guys! I ain't gonna repeat myself, so you'd better stop gabbing and hear what I gotta say. We've got a game in three weeks against McClaren's team from 56th Street and we'll need team jerseys before the . . . ."

Charlie interrupted, "Geez John, where the hell are we gonna get money to buy jerseys! My parents don't have it to spare, and I got nothin'."

Everyone murmured in agreement and looked back to John for an answer.

"If you'd wait a second, I'll tell you. We're gonna have a raffle. Everyone has gotta sell tickets."

Harry asked, "What're we gonna raffle?"

"That's where Morrie comes in."

"MORRIE, the crowd roared with laughter.

I asked myself, "Who the devil was Morrie, and what are they all laughing about?" My answer was a rotund ball of flab and freckles that stepped into the center of the crowd. As soon as I had arrived at the meeting and spotted this short, fat guy, I couldn't believe he was a football player and I learned he wasn't. The unhealthy looking blob was grinning from ear to ear must be Morrie. Listening to comments around me, I learned that Morrie was the neighborhood's shop-lifter par excellence. Morrie was so skilled that he had never been caught in his many thefts. To look at him, one would have to believe that larceny just might be the only thing he'd be good at.

John prompted, "Morrie, tell the guys about the prizes."

As soon as Morrie began to speak, it was painful to listen to him, because his voice approximated the sound of fingernails across a schoolroom's blackboard. Because of the passing traffic, Morrie tried to shout, and his shrill, scratchy voice became even more offensive.

"I can get my hands on a couple of small radios and . . ."

Charlie halted Morrie's pitch, "Where ya gettin the radios?"

"That's my business. I'm trying to help you guys. I'll get the radios in plenty of time for the drawing – don'tcha worry 'bout that."

It seems that that Morrie was also the Ludlow Street guys' punching bag, and he avoided more serious injuries by performing various favors for the gang members. You might say that Morrie was the Ludlow Gang's Shylock, and he suffered the same disrespect as Shakespeare's fictional character.

John took center stage again, "Okay, we'll have the raffle tickets by next Saturday. Come to practice at the Sanatorium's field at one o'clock, you'll get your tickets to sell, and we'll hold a practice for the game. Other than jerseys, everyone has to bring their own equipment: shoes, pads, helmets. Anybody got questions?"

"What if we ain't got anything? Charlie asked.

Frowning, John snarled, "Look, nobody here has a lot of football stuff, and I'm pretty damn sure most of you guys don't have the money to buy it. Guys we play won't be any better off than us. So . . . we'll play with what we got. Ya get it? See ya Saturday."

Everyone seemed to understand that was John's final word, and the group began to disperse to go their separate ways. I was left with some big concerns that if my parents should discover that the raffle prizes might be "hot," my tackle football days would be over. When it came to equipment, it was good to hear that others were in the same situation as I with no helmets, no pads, and no cleats. The lack of protection wasn't going to do my body much good. These thoughts were disrupted by Harry's voice.

"Hey Geordie, you're coming next Saturday aren't you?"

101

"Uh . . . sure . . . I'll be there."

"Great!"

John, smiling from ear to ear, called out, "See ya Saturday!"

"Okay, I'll see you."

Harry asked, "Ya wanna hang out with us awhile? We're heading for the drug store to get cokes or somethin'."

"Nah, I can't. I gotta deliver newspapers and I'm late already – Wolfie's gonna murder me."

John asked, "Wolfie? Who's Wolfie?"

"Ya don't want to know him. I'll see you next Saturday."

If I didn't get moving and fast, I knew that Wolfie would tear me up and down and I'd have to do a twenty pushup penalty or worse. I looked at my watch. Oh, Oh! I'd better run, or the Neighborhood Nazi would make me regret it. Fearing Wolfie's wrath, I tore back down 43rd Street.

CHAPTER FIFTEEN
MAD MAN MOUNTAIN

Leaping over the steps and through the open doorway into the branch office, I was relieved to see that the truck hadn't arrived with the papers. All the paper carriers, including my brother, Si were slumped on the benches along the wall.

"Whew! That's lucky [pant] – the papers haven't gotten here."
Si motioned for me to sit down beside him.
"Yeah, even luckier Wolfie hasn't noticed that you weren't here."
I crept over to Si and slipped down upon the hard, wooden bench.
"Where's he at?"
"He's in his office and he's real pissed that the truck's not here."
Just as I was about to tell Si about my meeting with the team, our three least favorite people, Ricky, Mickey and Peck came through the doorway. Their appearance in the branch office was a real shock to me. Not only did I dread the purpose of Ricky and Mickey's visit, but it was strange for them to be seen in the branch office. As soon as the two bullies spotted me, they strode across the room, menacing looks and all. A grinning Peck trailed safely behind Mickey. I wasn't worried about Peck, but Ricky and Mickey were big enough to kick my ass. Worst of all, I saw no reasonable avenue of escape.
Ricky shoved his fist in my face.
"There you are, you little bastard! If your old man thinks he can pick on us and get away with it, we'll show him."
Mickey growled, "Yeah, we'll show him after we get through with you, "How 'bout takin' a knuckle sandwich?"

Peck, still standing safely behind Mickey, sneered, "Yeh, yeh, yeh!"

Their threats were cut short, when a roar reverberated across the room.

"WHAT THE HELL ARE YOU BUMS DOING IN MY BRANCH?!"

Wolfie's booming voice caused the interlopers to wheel around and face the storming Nazi. It was obvious that they didn't know much about Wolfie, or else they would have left the premises on the dead run. It's possible that they were simply frozen by the sight, sound and fury of the crazed Kraut.

"Bu-Bu-Bu-Butt out! Ricky stammered. "We ain't got no beef with you!"

Ricky sputtered, "We . . . only want . . . to get a piece of this pu-punk. . .Geordie."

"Butt out? Butt out! IN MY BRANCH! Did you say BUTT OUT TO ME?"

"Yeah . . . eh," Ricky's bravado began to fade rapidly, when he got a closer look at Wolfie's bulging biceps and the Panzer commander's face distorted with rage.

"I don't give a *damn* what you're doing here! This is *my* branch and YOU'RE TRESPASSING!"

In a flash, Wolfie grabbed the backs of each of the intruders' shirt collars in a vise-like grip. Without missing a beat, my newfound savior marched and dragged Ricky and Mickey to the door. They hung helplessly like rag dolls in Wolfie's steel grip. The two managed only incoherent objections. With one forceful shove, Ricky and Mickey stumbled down the front steps and tumbled onto the pavement. Meanwhile, Peck had seen that things had taken an ugly turn, and had slipped out the door without Wolfie noticing him.

"DON'T COME BACK!"

Scrambling to his feet, Ricky shouted, "You're gonna be sorry!"

"Oh, really did you say?"

Wolfie made a feint forward as if he was coming down after them. That was enough for Ricky, Mickey and Peck. They took off like scared rabbits in full retreat up Locust Street.

When Wolfie returned to the room, he received a loud, standing ovation from all the newsboys, especially loud from Si and me. This had to be the first time that our Branch Captain had been recognized as anything but a tyrant. He seemed to enjoy the adulation, but only for an instant. In his desire to maintain absolute dominance over his carriers, Wolfie quickly returned to his Stalag Commandant's persona,

"I got a call from the office, and the truck will be an hour late today. Be back here in forty minutes. If anyone is late, they'll have to do forty push-ups with my boot in their rear!"

An hour later, Si and I, along with the other newsboys, dutifully returned on time. Still, the truck hadn't arrived, and the carriers began to grumble quietly among themselves. We were all bored and wanted to get onto our newspaper routes. Our mutterings of discontent ceased the moment Ricky and Mickey appeared again in the doorway. Grinning like a couple of Cheshire cats, the two strutted into the room. Peck had hesitated outside to make sure which way the wind might blow.

Si alerted the branch captain and shouted out, "Wolfie, they're back!"

"You're damn right we're back, you punk Jew," sneered Ricky.

"We're back, but we got somebody with us," cackled Mickey.

As if on cue, the doorway was darkened by something huge. It was the legendary Mad Man Mountain, a young man as wide as he was tall. My brother and I had only heard of the legend of Mad Man Mountain, but we had never seen the giant. There were plenty of stories of a Ludlow Gang member, who was as big as a Grizzly Bear and just as mean. One look at this monster before us, we were certain all the stories must be true and this must be the Mountain himself. Ricky and Mickey's were so determined to beat me up they had recruited the biggest and meanest guy in West Philly, Mad Man Mountain in person.

"DIDN'T I TELL YOU TWO NOT TO COME BACK!?"

All eyes shifted from the Mountain, when Wolfie's roar erupted from his office doorway. Wolfie sounded *really* pissed. He reached a new decibel level that made the wooden floor tremble. At first Wolfie hadn't noticed the giant in the doorway, since his eyes were focused on Ricky and Mickey.

"Well wise-guy, we've got someone here that you should meet," Ricky snickered, as he backed away from the oncoming Wolfie.

Taking refuge behind the huge man, Mickey laughed nervously and said, "Our buddy, Mad Man Mountain, is here to take care of you, while we beat the crap out of the Jew over there."

Without hesitation and no sign of fear, Wolfie strode directly up to the gorilla, chest to chest. He glared up defiantly at Mad Man's face that featured a fierce scowl and an extreme ugliness that only a mother could love.

Considering my options, I began to size up my survival prospects, but they didn't look good at the moment. Not even our very own Nazi could stand up against someone this big. Thoughts of escape seemed to be my only sensible strategy. Before any plans for flight could be put into action, I thought my ears were deceiving me. Wolfie had begun to laugh derisively at the Mountain. Was Wolfie nuts laughing in the giant's face?

"HA! HA! HA! What's a big tub of lard like you doing in my place?"

The Mountain couldn't believe Wolfie's scornful attitude toward him. Most people would cower and retreat. Instead of trembling before him, this little guy was laughing at him.

"You little son-of-a-bitch, I'm gonna eat you up and spit you out in little bits!"

Instead of being intimidated by a man a foot taller and almost 100 pounds heavier, Wolfie used surprise to his advantage and he sprang into action. Like lightning, the Nazi lunged forward, thrust his right arm under the Mountain's crotch and lifted the huge man onto his shoulders. It was a move that Wolfie must have seen at the Market Street Arena's wrestling matches.

All Mad Man could manage was a painful cry.

106

"HUH!" "OW!"

With the stunned behemoth sprawled as if paralyzed across his shoulders, Wolfie began to spin him around the room. Spectators' eyes opened wide in awe, seeing this huge person being overwhelmed like this.

While Wolfie spun his helpless victim around, all the Mountain could utter was a pained, "OOOOOOWWWWW!"

After several revolutions, Wolfie launched the huge man against the wall to his office.

CRASH!

The plasterboard wall gave way on impact, and Mountain fell through the wall with a resounding explosion. Ricky and Mickey couldn't believe what they had just seen done to their giant henchman. At the sound of the wall's collapse, I spotted Peck's nasty little face poke in from the doorway and disappear just as quickly. The wind hadn't blown well for Peck's cohorts, and Peck beat a hasty retreat home.

Seeing Mountain thrown through the office wall left no doubt in my mind that Wolfie, our very own Nazi, must be the strongest man in the world. Ricky and Mickey had never seen Mad Man Mountain lose a fight to anyone, not anyone. Wolfie scowled at the wall's huge hole. He didn't seem surprised at his own strength, but he was sure angry at the damage to his office's wall. Wolfie turned to take his rage out on Ricky and Mickey.

"Get that big piece of crap out of my office! Look at my wall, you *bastards*! Who's gonna pay for the repair of my office wall? It's a cinch that you three bums don't have a dime."

Legs spread apart, hands on his hips, Wolfie glared as Ricky and Mickey struggled to pull the dazed giant to his feet and back through the hole in the office's wall.

"If I ever see any one of you bums anywhere near my branch again, I'll break your goddamn necks," Wolfie shouted.

Defeated, dazed and limping badly, Mad Man Mountain was assisted out the door by Ricky and Mickey. I and all the newspaper boys were awestruck as Wolfie turned to face us. Absolute fear of our branch captain was replaced, at least for the moment, with deep respect. Instead of reveling in his victory, the delivery truck's arrival caught Wolfie's eye, and the Panzer commander returned in full force.

"The truck's here! Get your papers and get the hell out of here – I'm sick of looking at you punks!."

Wolfie counted out my papers and shoved them at me.

"You, it's your goddamn fault that those bastards came into my branch! Keep your damned arguments out of here! Do you understand me!?"

I could only nod vigorously. I wanted to thank Wolfie for saving me from Ricky and Mickey, but I thought better of it. One would not think to thank the Stalag Commandant for making his concentration camp a little nicer. My fellow carriers and I quietly left the branch that day, but the story, "Wolfie threw Mad Man Mountain through the branch office's wall," became a new West Philly legend.

CHAPTER SIXTEEN
SANDLOT FOOTBALL

My 49er teammates and I spread out across the area to sell raffle tickets. Within an eight block radius, for a week or more, every player's parent, relative, friend, neighbor, shopper, store owner, walker, church attendee were harassed and begged to buy a raffle ticket for an excellent chance to win a radio. There were some reports of kids being coerced to part with their lunch money in exchange for raffle tickets, but I can't say that I wasn't aware of or witness to any coercion or rough stuff.

"Hey lady, how-about supporting our football team and buy a raffle ticket to win a radio. They're only 20 cents a ticket, a dollar for five."

"Hey mister, help our team get jerseys and buy a raffle ticket for a terrific prize, a radio."

When I approached my mother to buy raffle tickets, she bought five tickets and expressed her pleasure that my team and I were engaged in a worthwhile effort.

"It's good and I'm truly surprised that your friends are raising money for football jerseys in a legitimate way."

As long as Mom appeared satisfied, I was happy to keep it that way, but I still had qualms over selling raffle tickets for someone's chance to win a radio of unknown origin. I was able to keep my uneasiness and moralistic principles in check, because the lure of the football team and a team jersey was too great. As long as raffle ticket buyers and my parents were satisfied, no one was really being hurt. Who knows, Morrie might have a legitimate way to get his hands on a couple of radios. Morrie had said, "Where and how I get the radios is my business."

By the time the second weekend practice was held, sufficient money had been raised from the raffle tickets' sales. John brought the jerseys to the practice field and proudly presented them to the team. The jerseys were blue with white shoulders and white numerals. I rushed forward to grab the number 29 jersey and slipped it over my head.

I shouted, "Boy, this looks great!"

With the team outfitted with jerseys, the 49ers began to look like a football team. About six team members had some sort of a plastic or leather helmet, and a few had shoulder pads. The twins, whose father owned the local bar, were the only ones that came fully equipped with helmets, rib and hip pads, regulation pants with knee and thigh pads, and football cleats. With my newspaper money, my first purchase was a pair of football cleats and a week later I bought a blue, plastic helmet with a white stripe. Most of the players wore old sneakers and long threadbare pants.

Team practices were held on the fenced-in, private, sanatorium's grounds. We were liable to be chased off the grounds at any time, but it was the largest, flat piece of ground around. It wasn't much of a field for football. There were scattered patches of grass and weeds, but mostly bare, rocky spots that created horrendous, painful, brush burns. The area was long enough, but not quite wide enough to be a regulation football field. Along one side, a steep slope ran up from the field to the sanatorium's buildings.

During practices, it wasn't uncommon to see a patient in pajamas race across the grounds with men in white coats in hot pursuit. On some occasions, among the spectators at practices, an escaped asylum's inmate would be spotted in bare feet and a bath robe. Some practices were abbreviated, when the police were summoned by the sanatorium's administration, "Get those kids off our grounds!"

When practices began, John's older brother, Butch, had elected himself as coach. Butch worked on a beer truck and had little to none football experience, but because he was older and bigger than any of the 49er players he became coach. Due to his lack of football knowledge, Butch designed simple plays with little strategy or technique: "John, hand Geordie the ball, Geordie runs right, and the rest of you guys knock the shit out of the bums in front of you.

It was many years before television's ESPN and football analysts. If there was a book on football strategy, no one could afford to buy one, so the players, having no better football knowledge, followed our so-called coach's directions.

John became the team's T formation quarterback, even though he wanted to be the fullback. It didn't take long before John and everyone else realized that the fullback slot wasn't right for him. Even though he was big and strong, John ran like he wore army boots, even when he wasn't wearing army boots. Because of his size and arm strength, John had to be satisfied to be our quarterback. I was picked to be the primary running back, Harry and Smitty were the two ends, Rinny was the center, Charlie and the twins, Jack and Wally, were our linemen. Others were tried in the backfield, but ended up in the line. It soon became evident that I was the team's only legitimate running back.

Practices were disorganized, rough and tumble and more like rugby scrums than football. To my mother's horror, I consistently returned home from practices with a scratched up face and a bloody nose. Because helmets in those years didn't have face bars or masks, there was no protection for my face from headlong tackles into the ball carrier. There wasn't a practice that I wouldn't receive some fierce looking, cherry- red abrasion on an elbow, knee, or a bloody nose. My injuries only added to my mother's fears and complaints.

Finally and thankfully, game day arrived and none too soon for me, because Mom's objections to my injuries were mounting in intensity. She repeatedly expressed her concerns that one might expect from a Jewish mother, but concerns that would prove to be eerily prophetic:

"Oy, Vai iz mir, you haven't played a game yet and look at you – you're battered and bruised! There's no telling what else can happen to you."

Now, it was time for the 49ers to batter someone else. The game with the Falcons was held on the sanatorium field. Pop had promised that he'd keep an eye on me and paced the sidelines with my brothers and players' friends and family. Pop had taken time off from his work to be at almost every practice, since the city's radio shop was only a half a block up Market Street. Si and Gadget were among the most vociferous rooters on the 49ers' side of the field. They started shouting well before the game's start.

The sidelines were unmarked, except for a few articles of clothing laid down to indicate out of bounds and goal lines. First downs were measured by using two broomstick handles and a length of rope that stretched to ten yards or so. This was the truest and crudest form of sandlot football.

The 49ers and our opponents had arrived at the field in ones and twos. As some of the players for both teams began to dress for the game, I looked across to the other sideline and noted that the Falcons players weren't any better equipped with football equipment. Everyone had some sort of plastic or leather helmet. A few on each team were fully equipped for football and only about half had shoulder pads. Charlie had warned the team that there was the possibility that the Falcons' McClaren might throw in a few "ringers", which wouldn't be unusual for sandlot football.

Sandlot games were only a small step above pickup games and absent of restrictions as to the age, size or weight of the players. The sandlot game rules were limited to the scant knowledge of the players and spectators, and the absence of real referees could only lead to chaos. Fortunately, our Falcon opponents seemed to be fielding a team without ringers, which was some small relief to me.

"There's McClaren," John pointed across the field to a tall, rangy figure. "He's big and fast, and he'll be tough to bring down,"

Smitty asked John. "Where are these guys from?"

"They call themselves the 56th Street Falcons. That's all I know."

I watched as John and Butch went out to the middle of the field to greet McClaren and some other big guy, McClaren's older brother. McClaren's brother and Butch agreed to act as referees. At this point, I was trying as hard as I could to overcome my stomach's raging butterflies. The coin was tossed and the Falcons elected to receive. When John returned to the team's huddle on our sidelines, he looked around at the team's eager faces.

"We kick off. Let's get out there and knock the crap outta somebody!"

I swallowed real hard and ran onto the field with the team. Since we couldn't afford a football tee, Harry kneeled and held the ball upright with the tip of his finger while John advanced to kick the ball. He gave it a pretty good boot downfield. McClaren picked up the ball on one bounce somewhere around an unidentified twenty-yard- line, without yard markers it was hard to say. With the ball tucked under his arm, the tall, speedy runner began to head straight up the field, while my teammates and I rumbled down the field, bearing down on the ball carrier. Smitty ran down the field's left side and was cut down with a crushing cross-body block, clearing the way for the runner's cut to the sideline.

Galloping down the center of the field, I avoided a block and spotted McClaren's move to the outside. Instinctively, I took an angle that would allow me to intercept the runner. McClaren was so intent on eyeing an open path to the goal line he failed to see me closing in on him.

BAM!

The force of my unexpected blow to his knees knocked McClaren head over heels, out of bounds on about the 49ers' forty-yard line. McClaren came up sputtering.

"WHAT IN THE HELL!"

The runner spun around to see what hit him. When he saw me get to my feet, a look of astonishment turned quickly to one of disgust. The Falcon captain pointed a menacing finger at me.

"Who are you? Forget it . . . I don't care who the hell you are - that's the last time you tackle me."

Teammates ran up to me and pounded my back.

"Way to go, Geordie!"

The 49ers lined up in some sort of a defensive formation as the Falcons went back to huddle. Butch, our coach, now a referee, knew as much about defensive schemes as he knew offensive tactics. The only defensive strategy he preached was, "Line up against somebody and kill the guy with the ball."

Speaking loudly in the huddle, a furious McClaren could be heard pleading to his team.

"For Christ's sake, block that little son-of-a-bitch!"

The Falcons broke out of the huddle and set down in a single wing formation with McClaren in the tailback position, and he began to call the signals.

"Hut one . . . Hut two!"

On the two-count, the ball spiraled back to McClaren, and he began to lope around right end. Smitty, our defensive end, was blocked to the inside. From the middle linebacker position, I closed on McClaren and hit the runner with an effective shoestring tackle. McClaren lurched forward and fell facedown at the line of scrimmage for no gain. Again, McClaren fumed to see that I was his tackler. He ran back to the Falcon huddle, arms waving, screaming all the way at his teammates.

"I TOLD YOU'SE GUYS TO BLOCK THAT PUNK!"

The more McClaren screamed, the more my confidence and aggressiveness grew. In the Falcons huddle, McClaren was so mad and he talked so loudly I knew that he would carry the ball again. The thoroughly pissed off Falcon captain took the snap.

This time, he began to run around left end. Harry avoided a block, but grabbed nothing but air as McClaren shed his tackle attempt with a straight arm and galloped to the sideline. McClaren was certain he'd score this time, but I was able to avoid two blockers and came up to bounce the runner out of bounds at the thirty-five yard line, a gain of only five yards. McClaren was livid. He returned to the huddle red faced, and berated his team.

"DAMMIT! WHY CAN'T YOU BLOCK THAT BASTARD?!"

By third down, I had grown sick of the Falcon captain's whining and name-calling. Without defensive signals from our coach, who was acting as a referee, I knew it was a sure passing situation, and I decided to rush the passer in emulating the NFL Eagles' Wild Man Willy. McClaren received the snap from center and back pedaled. In preparing to pass, he focused on his receivers down field, but McClaren failed to notice that I was bearing down on his blind side.

"OOF!"

McClaren's breath escaped with the force of my headlong tackle into his mid-section. The ball bounced out of the passer's hand and rolled crazily across the field. There ensued a mad scramble for the ball. John's strength allowed him to shove everyone aside, and he pounced on the fumble. In the meantime, I had landed in a sitting position on top of McClaren's chest.

"GET THE HELL OFF ME YOU SON OF A BITCH!" McClaren shouted, almost in tears.

It's hard to explain my emotion at that moment, but my reaction to his insults and McClaren's incessant whining was spontaneous. In an attempt to extricate myself from the writhing and bitching McClaren, instead of merely pushing off, I sort of punched down on the whiner's chest. Considering that this was the first punch I had ever thrown at anyone, I was as just as surprised as McClaren. I imagine the violence in football had unleashed aggressions that were dormant in me until now.

McClaren screamed, "OWWW!"

115

My punch might have been no more than a hefty stiff-arm than a punch, and McClaren was probably more shocked than hurt. He exploded to his feet, let out a howl, and rushed at me with blood in his eyes. In the struggle to recover the fumble, there were no witnesses to my punch. The Falcon's scream and charge at me brought Charlie and John to quickly intervene and held McClaren at bay.

"HE PUNCHED ME!"

McClaren roared with tears of anger, jumping up and down, and desperate to get at me. Charlie and John pushed away the fuming, frustrated, and seemingly deranged Falcon captain.

"You're full of crap, Geordie wouldn't punch anyone," John shouted.

John couldn't believe that his mild mannered Jew would do such a thing. McClaren's accusation couldn't even be believed by his own teammates as I stood with an innocent look on my face.

"I'm tellin' you, the son of a bitch sucker-punched me!"

After several minutes of shoving and exchange of curses, the two teams separated, but McClaren was still raving, insisting, "I'm gettin' even with that son of a bitch!"

In the 49ers huddle, John whispered to me, "You really didn't punch him, did you?"

"Naah." My upper lip curled up ever so slightly with my response.

At first, the 49ers' players looked over at me. Then, we looked at each other. All at once, the entire huddle erupted into raucous laughter. As the huddle's laughter began to subside, John cocked his head to one side and took a long and thoughtful look at me. It's as if he was seeing me for the very first time. The team captain smiled knowingly and winked at me, and I winked back. John nodded, smiled to himself, and returned his attention to the game.

"Shaddup you guys – let's get back to football. Now, it's our turn. Center the ball to me on three and I'll pitch it to Geordie. You take it around right end. Everybody, *block* your man."

The 49ers broke the huddle and lined up in a T formation.

Under center, John hollered signals, "Hut one . . . Hut two . . . Hut three!"

Taking the center's snap, John peeled to the right and made a perfect leading pitch to me. His lateral caught me in full stride and allowed me to turn the right corner. Harry made a clean block to seal off the defensive end's move that gave me a clear path to the sideline. The Falcons' safety, McClaren, was the only Falcon between goal line and me, and he was determined to punish me with a horse-collar tackle. The would-be tackler came up too fast and I gave him a leg, which left McClaren swinging an arm wildly in a lunge at my neck. With a juke, the Falcon hit nothing but air, and stumbled to the turf. I sailed free across the sneaker-marked goal line and scored the first touchdown of my sandlot football career. My teammates were ecstatic and bounded like crazy kangaroos, all the way down the field to join me for an end zone celebration.

The rest of the half was scoreless. On defense, I continued to enjoy tackling and frustrating McClaren. On one tackle, I felt a strange, sharp pain in my left thigh, but thought nothing more of it, probably another brush burn, I thought. When on offense, I gained positive yardage on every play, but was unable to break free for another long gain. After my touchdown, we played the rest of the half more like a rugby scrum than football, and neither team gained an advantage.

During the break at halftime, Harry looked across the field and shouted to John.

"John, d'ya see what the Falcons are doin'? They're giving those big guys their jerseys and equipment."

I looked across the field to see that our fear of ringers was being realized. The Falcons' bigger, older brothers and friends were putting on pads and jerseys. Butch walked up to John and said, "Tell your guys to take off their pads, helmets and jerseys. We ain't gonna let those bastards get away with that shit."

From that point on, my teammates and I didn't get a chance to play the entire second half. All we could do was watch the bigger, older guys wrestle and hammer each other in a disorganized brawl that had no semblance of football. Since the two officials, that had refereed the first half, were now in the game and playing opposite each other, there was no control over the mayhem that ensued. Each play ended with arguments, pushing, piling on and an exchange of punches. What it was *wasn't* football. Brass knuckles and bats were the only things missing from this miserable spectacle.

Mercifully, someone with a watch declared that time was up, and Butch and the rest of the 49ers' bruised ringers separated themselves from their equally battered ringer foes. Our team replacements staggered off the field with multiple scrapes and scratches, bloody noses, swollen eyes, torn and blood splattered clothing.

I was disappointed to see my first tackle football game taken away from my teammates and me, and I stood dejectedly on the sidelines. I shuddered to think what my father would say. The sad affair's outcome was a mere bump in the road to John and most of the 49ers loudly declared victory.

"HOORAY! WE WON!"

My team claimed the win, since they had the only official score in the first half. I was flabbergasted at their joyfulness and their logic. How could they be so happy and I was so disappointed? I didn't play a down in the second half.

My father and brothers joined me in walking off the field and out onto Market Street, listening to the Eagles chants:

"WHOOPEE! WE WON! WE WON!"

This declaration of victory aggravated the Falcons:

"LIKE HELL YOU DID!"

On the walk home, I could see that Pop was upset.

"Don't tell your mother how this thing ended. I don't think she'd understand and it'd only upset her. But you've *got* to tell your team that they shouldn't play with ringers. They should refuse to play, if another team pulls that stunt."

118

"You bet I won't tell Mom. It sure wasn't fun not to play the second half . . . OWW!"

I felt a sharp pain in my left leg.

"Pop, my leg really hurts."

"Can you walk on it?"

"Yeah, but it still hurts."

Si asked, "Where's it hurt, Geordie?"

"Right here," I pointed to my left thigh.

Now, my father grew concerned, "I'll take a look at it, when we get home."

We continued our walk home, but I began to walk more gingerly. Each step caused a burning, stinging pain in my thigh. Pop led us into the house and called out.

"We're home!"

From the kitchen, Mom called back, "Is Geordie all right?"

"Don't worry Fan, he's fine."

Wiping her hands on her apron, my concerned mother appeared from the kitchen.

"Are you sure you're all right? You don't look all right to me."

By now, my thigh was beginning to really ache, and I couldn't prevent my voice from wavering and my face from grimacing.

"Yeah Mom, I'm . . . Okay,"

"You say Okay, but why are you making that face and with that voice?"

"I'm not making a face. Honest Mom, I'm Okay.

"Don't tell me you're Okay. A mother knows not Okay, when she sees it. Well, George did they win?"

"Uh . . . yeah I think they won."

"You think, what does that mean?"

"Sorry Mom, I'd better go take a bath and change my clothes."

Without another word, I began to climb the stairway, and did my best not to show I was in pain. Each step generated progressively greater pain, but I clenched my teeth to prevent a cry that would have surely alarmed my mother. Once in my bedroom and anxious to see the cause of the stinging sensation, I

119

noticed a tear in my pants in about the same location as the pain. As soon as I removed my pants, I got a clear sickening look at a long, deep, gaping gash on my thigh that had layers of flesh and fatty tissue exposed.

"Pop . . . can you come up here?" .

Recognizing a distress signal in my voice, a concerned father clambered up the stairs two at a time. One quick glance at the wound, he didn't hesitate for a second.

"C'mon we're going to the emergency room."

"Will I need stitches?"

"Stitches, you bet you do! Get your pants back on. We're going . . . *now*!"

Descending the stairs, we were met by my alarmed Mother.

"George, what's the matter?"

"He needs stitches in his thigh and I've got to get him to Penn's emergency room right away."

"Oy, Vai iz mir! I knew no good could come from playing football with those horrible ruffians."

We left the house in the wake of a fusillade of recriminations.

CHAPTER SEVENTEEN
THE EMERGENCY ROOM

The Number 42 trolley rolled down Spruce Street and carried Pop and me to the stop at the University of Pennsylvania's hospital, just across from the university's main campus.

We entered an overflowing emergency room of misery. The large room was jammed with a chorus of weeping children, ugly coughs, anguished faces, and a woeful variety of all too visible injuries. After registering me for treatment, my father sat down beside me in the last vacant chair. We had plenty of time to stew over Mom's scolding that she issued with a biting English accent and spiced with a large helping of Yiddish.

After an hour's wait in this atmosphere of suffering and distress, which seemed like an absolute eternity to me, my name was called. Pop and I were led by a pretty nurse dressed all in white, across a white, linoleum floor, down a white walled corridor into a brightly lit, white room.

"Mr. Eaton, where exactly is your injury?"

"It's on my left thigh."

"Alright then, please take off your trousers and sit up on this table."

Off went my trousers.

The nurse needed just a glance at my leg to say, "Yes, sure enough, the doctor needs to see you. He'll be with you shortly."

An hour later, a young, spectacled, male doctor in a white coat swept into the room

"Well now, what's the problem young man?"

Pointing to the gash, "I've got a cut right here on my left thigh doctor."

"Hmmm, let me take a look at that. My, my . . . that's a pretty deep cut. How'd it happen?"

121

"I don't know. I was playing football and didn't see it till I got home."

"This is going to take a few sutures. Have you had a tetanus shot?"

"I think so. A couple of years ago, when a dog bit my finger."

The doctor leaned over to take a closer look at the cut. "You know, this could have been caused by a piece of glass or even a knife."

Pop frowned.

"Did you say knife, doctor?"

"Yeah, it's possible. The laceration is clean, straight and deep. In any case, we'll clean this up, sew it and your son should be fine."

The wound was cleaned and stitched in quick order.

On the trolley ride back home, we steeled ourselves for the resumption of Mom's wrath. Her fears were well founded and the scolding went on for days.

A week later, Pop escorted me back to the hospital's emergency room to have the stitches removed. After another interminable wait among the emergency room's miseries, a male orderly escorted Pop and me to another white, brightly lit room.

"Wait here for the doctor," the orderly said and left.

Thirty minutes later, an attractive female intern in a long white coat entered the room, a stethoscope draped around her neck.

"Good morning, young Mr. Eaton. I understand you need to have your sutures removed."

"Yes, doctor."

"Fine, now let me take a look." The pretty, young doctor bent down and went nose to nose with me. She gazed long and hard into my eyes. I couldn't understand why the doctor was peering so intently in my eyes, and Pop was about to question her, when the intern stood up, visibly exasperated.

"I *don't* see them."

Pop asked, "See what doctor?"

"I don't see the stitches in your son's eye."

I smiled and Pop couldn't help but laugh.

Now, the intern was really confused.

"What's so funny?"

I giggled, "The stitches are in my thigh, not my eye."

The doctor's pretty face reddened a beautiful shade of crimson. She reached for my chart, sputtered and tried real hard to suppress a giggle. "The nurse must have told me the stitches were in your thigh, and I thought she said eye."

On return from the hospital, I remained determined to continue playing football with the 49ers. In the following days, there was much discussion about my future in football. Mom remained diametrically opposed to me resuming play with those "hooligans." My two brothers could have easily swayed a vote that would have doomed my football play with the 49ers, but fortunately, their votes didn't count. Pop remained my ally and convinced Mom to let me play, but the agreement was extremely fragile. For the time being, I remained eligible to play football with the 49ers in our next game.

CHAPTER EIGHTEEN
THE KNOCKOUT

The Falcons demanded a rematch and the game was to be played on Passon's Field, an almost barren lot, diagonally across 48th Street from West Philadelphia High school. Passon's Field was an even poorer excuse for a football site than the sanatorium. Even the high school refrained from using the "field" for any athletic purpose, because it was all dirt, rocks, tin cans, broken glass and scattered clumps of weeds. West Philly High had plans to develop the grounds for athletics, but that wasn't expected to happen for years. Because no one would chase us off of Passon's, and it was large enough for a regulation football field, the Falcons had designated this godforsaken piece of ground for its rematch with the 49ers.

On game day, the team gathered in front of my house, waiting for a ride to the game. Pop had volunteered to drive the entire team to the game in his ancient, 1928 Packard that resembled a battleship more than an automobile. Even though, the vehicle was enough of a monstrosity, my father added to its grotesqueness by painting the ancient Packard a dull Battleship Gray from an old can of deck paint he had used to paint the front porch's flooring. Because the aged Packard had no rings left on its pistons, the car burned more oil than gasoline and belched a trail of acrid smoke. It was a sure-fire, rolling, attention-getter and a major source of embarrassment for my siblings and me. Embarrassed by the attention and amusement created by the passing of our family's gray monster, my brothers, sisters and I would scrunch down in our seats, hoping not to be identified by friends or even noticed by strangers. Invariably, ridicule was heaped upon us as we passed people on the street, and a common derisive shout was heard.

124

"GET A HORSE!"

The old gray beast had one advantage in its ability to carry the entire 49ers football team and my brothers, to our game with the Falcons. This attribute was of little solace to me-I hated the Packard with a passion. I knew we couldn't afford a new car, but if I had my druthers, I would have been happy to walk to the game.

"John, when are we gonna have the raffle for the radios?" Harry asked.

"I haven't seen Morrie or the radios."

"Gee, John, people are asking me about the raffle."

"Me too," others in the group spoke up.

"Why ask me anyway - have any of you bums seen him?"

My eyes were diverted from the conversation, when I spotted Pop coming down the front steps.

"Pssst . . . My father's coming. Shut up about it!"

Fortunately, Pop didn't hear the talk about Morrie and the radios. There'd be hell to pay, if he realized we were discussing Morrie's disappearance and the missing raffle prizes. But where was Morrie? That was a good question.

Somehow, the entire 49ers' team with their football gear squeezed into our vintage Packard. As the Packard pulled away from the curb, the team let out a huge cheer, immediately followed by groans from bodies crushing bodies. In between groans, grunts, and laughs, the passengers exchanged gibes and curses. When the old Packard pulled up at the Locust Street side of Passon's Field, Pop shouted.

"OKAY . . . EVERYONE OUT!"

Like one of the circus' funniest circus clown acts, we all rolled out of the Packard laughing, screaming, and landing in a ball of humanity on the pavement. Seeing the wild and weird arrival of the 49ers team, McClaren, my nemesis, left his team's warmups to greet us.

Snickering, the Falcon captain said to John, "Ya got any ringers?

"No. Do you got any wise guy? .

Spotting me, McClaren strutted over and stopped to face me, hands on his hips, and sneered, "I hear you got cut. Tch . . . Tch."

John stepped between us, "What's it to you?"

McClaren's smirk was as evil as his words.

"You never can tell what might happen today."

John snarled, "If you're the son-of-a-bitch that cut Geordie, you'll get yours."

I had suspected McClaren, but his threat made me certain that he was the one who cut my leg. I looked at him with disgust and walked away without a word, but I was determined to make him pay . . . in the game . . . on every tackle.

"Hey look over there!" Smitty shouted. "That's Shoeless Reds – the little guy with no shoes. He's one tough cookie."

Harry cursed, "Damn! Smitty, you're right. The bastards promised not to use older guys, but they just went out and picked up one of the toughest and fastest players anywhere around."

I peered over to the other sideline to see this "tough cookie." What I saw was a little fireplug of a guy, red hair sprouting out from beneath his helmet, and . . . my gosh . . . he was running in his bare feet.

"Hey! He's not wearing shoes."

John placed his meaty paw on my shoulder.

"You're right. Reds don't wear shoes, when he plays. He's faster than hell and he's built so low to the ground that he's tough as crap to bring down. Geordie, ya gotta go low on him. If you try to tackle him high, he's gone!"

On our first possession, John passed to Harry in the left flat and Harry ran for thirty yards before being tackled viciously by shoeless Reds. On the next play, I bulled up the middle and was jarred by the high-low tackles of McClaren and Reds.

"Take that you little punk," taunted McClaren.

I hadn't yet learned to run into the line with my head up that would have allowed me the ability to spot openings for cuts to the

126

right or left. When I bulled with my head down through an opening in the line created by good blocks, I was unable to see the opportunity to cut to either sidelines. Even so, on the next play, I kept my legs churning and carried the ball ten yards and a first down. On ensuing plays, I chalked up yardage running around right end, making the corner at left end, and slashing through right tackle for the final five yards and a touchdown.

After crossing the goal line, I walked past McClaren, pretending my nemesis wasn't there. McClaren, angered by the touchdown and even madder at me for ignoring him, shoved me in the back. Taken by surprise, I stumbled forward, but managed to regain my footing.

McClaren sneered, "You were just lucky this time punk."

Before I had a chance to react, McClaren walked away laughing. I vowed to myself that somehow I had to get even with this guy.

Shoeless Reds lived up to his billing. When it was the Falcons turn to run its offense, it was Reds that carried the load, not McClaren. On the Falcons first two downs, my tackle attempts of Reds were too high, and I only managed to slow him down. As hard as I tried I couldn't seem able to get low enough to tackle his legs. The little runner broke free from my attempts, tackle after tackle attempt, I found he was like a human bowling ball. On the Falcons' first offensive series, Reds scored and tied the game.

Without real referees, the game was punctuated with cheap shots, late blocks and tackles, piling on, and it only got rougher as the game progressed. Almost every play ended with the exchange of curses and pushing and shoving. The so-called referees, a supporter from each team, argued as much as the players. I just wanted to play football and stayed clear of the disputes. Each time McClaren carried the football, I made an all-out effort to hit him as hard as I could with bone-rattling "sticks."

Even though I was considered a good tackler, my technique was faulty. Instead of using my shoulders as the primary force, too often I used my helmet as a battering ram. The tackled felt the impact, but I the tackler, felt the collisions with sounds of bells ringing in my head. After one particularly hard, head-butt tackle, McClaren lay moaning, flat on his back. I got to my feet staggering and listening to a pretty tune that sounded a lot like *The Bells of Saint Mary*.

Charlie came up to me, shaking his head, and said, "Geordie, that was hell of tackle, but don'tcha know that you gotta hit with your shoulders, not your head. Ya gotta be punchy?"

Smitty chortled, "Yo, that's a good nickname for Geordie. We'll call him Punchy."

A nickname was born that was much to my deep dismay. The entire 49ers' team embraced the nickname and chanted, "Punchy, Punchy, Punchy." I forced a thin smile, but I instantly hated the name, "Punchy." It was just then I fully appreciated how much my little brother detested his unflattering nickname, "Gadget."

The second half began with the score still tied. Fortunately, there wasn't a repeat of the previous game's entrance of the ringers. Both teams stuck to their agreement that older guys weren't permitted on either team.

Early in the second half, we had taken over on downs on our own forty-yard line. Without yard line markings, the best guess would be somewhere around the forty-yard line. John faked the ball to the fullback into the line and pitched to me on the run. Smitty made a beautiful undercutting block on the defensive end, Charlie cut down the outside linebacker, McClaren. The blocks allowed me to skirt the right end and break free down the sidelines. Reds had gone for the fake and belatedly saw me heading for the goal line. The barefooted speedster ran like the wind to catch me at the invisible goal line, identified only by an old boot on either sideline. When Reds hit me high from the side, I spun around to stretch across the goal line as I fell. Did I score? With an invisible goal line, it was hard to say for sure, and a controversy was bound to erupt.

The entire 49ers' team ran up to me to celebrate the touchdown, but the Falcon's team was just as certain that I hadn't

128

scored. A loud argument began, punctuated by unkind mentions of parentage. The loudest of the protestors was McClaren himself.

"Bull shit! That's no goddamn touchdown! He never crossed the goal line!"

Instead of attempting to mediate the argument or make a ruling, the useless referees stood outside the circle of players and argued with each other. Charlie, the only weight lifter on our team, entered the circle, chest out, hands at his side, and stuck his jaw inches from McClaren's red face.

Charlie challenged McClaren, "It *was* a touchdown, or do you want to *fight* about it?"

McClaren spit back, "You bet I . . . "

BONG!

McClaren didn't have a chance to complete his sentence. Without a second's hesitation, Charlie had unleashed a sweeping, lightning bolt, devastating uppercut that struck square on McClaren's jaw. The force from Charlie's punch lifted McClaren's feet clear off of the ground, and his body fell straight back landing like an axed oak tree, out like a light. Everyone stood in stunned silence, eyes popped, and mouths agape. Finally recovering from their shock at the suddenness and power of Charlie's knockout punch, two Falcons' teammates rushed over to the motionless body.

"He's still breathin'!"

A few moments later, McClaren showed signs of life.

"[Cough], [moan]. Where am I?"

Eventually, McClaren was helped to his feet, but his legs acted like they were made of rubber. The Falcons looked at us and we looked at them. Not a word was spoken. Everyone realized that the game was over and headed off the field.

John and Charlie walked up to me and smiled.

Charlie said, "That was for you Punch."

I hadn't looked for any help, and I believed that I'd gotten some pretty good licks in on McClaren with hard tackles, but I had to appreciate John and Charlie's good intentions. Their feeling that they had to avenge me made me realize that these guys weren't just my team-mates, they had become friends and protectors.

On the way back to the Packard, the 49ers' team began to chant.

"WE WON . . . WE WON!"

Again, a declaration of victory was of little satisfaction to me. Here it was my second football game and both games were incomplete. One game was taken over by the older guys and the other ended midway in a fight.

"Way to go, Punchy! You won us another game," John and the others cheered.

It was nice to hear the praise, but I cringed at the name, "Punchy." The ride back to Forty-Fourth Street was a joyous one. The 49ers laughed and cheered over their second victory. Sitting by my Pop, I saw that he was stone-faced, his teeth were clenched, and he hadn't spoken a word. I realized that my father wasn't any happier about this game than I was.

When we reached our home's front door, Pop held his arm out to prevent me from entering the house. In low tones he said, "Sunshine, I don't like what's going on in these games. Someone can get seriously hurt and I'm not going to permit you to play with that crowd, if the games can't be better controlled. If your mother hears about this, your football days are over. Do you understand?"

"Yep, I do."

I was just as disillusioned as my father. Not only was the game cut short, but I picked up a lousy nickname.

That evening, at the dinner table, the normal family conversations went on:

"Helen, did you get your Calculus test results back?" The mother asked.

"I got an A+ Mom."

130

Si teased, "I thought you said you flunked that test?"

Mom frowned at Si and turned to me. "Geordie, how did the game go?"

"Okay."

Gadget exclaimed, "He scored two touchdowns, but the game ended in a fight!"

Why did my brother mention the word "fight?"

"WHAT!" . . . a fight!" My Mother's greatest fears had been realized.

"It's okay Fannie. Geordie wasn't involved in the fight. Two boys got into an argument, that's all."

Pop's explanation didn't soothe Mom's concern, but it only managed to reduce the volume of her objections.

"I told you that they're nothing but ruffians."

"I'm fine Mom. I didn't get hurt and *I* didn't fight anybody. The 49ers are really good guys and they stuck up for me."

Pop got up from his seat, walked over to Mom, put his arm around her shoulder and kissed her on the cheek. This seemed to settle the matter for the moment. The dinner and the football discourse ended without further incident. I was happy that my football days weren't over, but I was beginning to have my own misgivings about playing sandlot football.

CHAPTER NINETEEN
TOOTSIE TAKES CENTER

After school, in the week after the fight-ending-game, our neighborhood crowd gathered on Sam's steps. Tootsie and Jane had joined us guys and listened intently to my recount of the game. Tootsie had never seen a football game, not even a high school game, because her Evangelist father objected to all forms of violence, including football.

Tootsie said, "Golly, I don't know anything about football. What's a formation? I guess I mean what's a T formation?"

I couldn't believe that she had never seen a football game.

"Okay Tootsie, there's an offensive line of seven guys and four backs in the shape of a T. The quarterback stands right behind the center, and the center hikes the ball into the quarterback's hands."

"A hike is what? Can you show me?"

"Nope, I don't think so."

"Please, please, Geordie,"

"Oh . . . Okay Tootsie, just keep your girl britches on. Don't get excited, it's not a big deal. You be the center and hike the ball back to me, when I say two."

First, I had to show Tootsie the proper crouched center's stance and how to hold the tilted ball with two hands. Then, I took up the quarterback's position directly behind her. So far, the instruction was going well. Everyone was giggling, including Tootsie. That is, until I innocently placed the back of my left hand low and against an unsuspecting Tootsie's rear end.

"WHOOPS!" Tootsie let out a shriek and jumped three feet in the air.

"WHA . . . what did I do!? I shouted throwing my hands in the air.

I was flabbergasted at Tootsie's reaction to my touch and stumbled back. I had no clue why she would jump like that. What did I do?

Jane shouted, "GEORDIE . . . YOU DUMMY! You can't do that to a *girl*!"

Don and Bob were in hysterics. My brothers weren't sure what had just transpired, but laughed anyway. Tootsie's face was as red as a beet. As if her feet were on fire, she screamed and jumped up and down in optimal embarrassment. All I could do was stand dumbfounded and had no idea what to say or do. With all the ridicule being heaped on me, I understood I must have done something wrong and I became completely flustered and frustrated.

Mercifully, Harry arrived at that moment to break up a mortifying experience for Tootsie and me

"Geordie, we got another game this Saturday with a different team. They've got some really good players, so we got Reds to play for us."

"The little shoeless guy we just played against?"

"Yep, he's a good guy, we needed another running back, and he'll take some of the load off of you."

"I guess that's okay with me, but I'm not sure about my Mom. We sure as heck better play a full game this time. You know my mother's against me playing, and my Pop has about had it. If there's another fight, I'm off the team for sure."

"John talked to these guys. They guaranteed us that there'd be no trouble. Oh, by the way, we think Morrie's in jail."

"What are we going to do about the raffle?"

"The raffle's been held."

"Who won the radios?"

"Some guys won. We got our jerseys, and nobody's saying anything."

"That's [Cough] sounds to me dishonest as hell," Don said.

"Hey, Don butt out – it's none of your damn business!"

133

The news about the radios and raffle was bad news. I had to warn my brothers, "Don't let our parents know about this. I'd be off the team for sure."

Si scowled and shook his head from side to side.

"We won't say anything, but it's looking more and more like you shouldn't be messing with those guys,"

Billy pretended to button his lips, but didn't look any happier than Si.

"I know, I know, but I want to play football and this is my only chance."

"You'll be s-o-r-r-r-r-y," Billy taunted.

"Shaddup, Gadget," Harry snarled.

Having had a bad experience with Tootsie and hearing enough abuse from my brothers, I escaped from the group, but still determined to play football.

"Harry, I'll try to be there. I'll play, if my parents will let me."

CHAPTER TWENTY
PAIN IN THE NECK

It was game day with the Baltimore Bears. "Who was on the Bears team? No one knew and no one would know until the moment we faced the other team. As my brothers and I approached the gate to the Sanatorium's field, I proudly carried my newly purchased shoulder pads, along with my helmet and football cleats. Because I had left doubt with Harry that my parents might not let me play, I toyed with the idea of making a grand entrance onto the field. I thought I'd surprise everybody they'd be relieved to see me. It didn't quite work out as intended.

"The last time I talked to Harry, I told him I wasn't sure Mom would let me play. I bet they'll be surprised – I'm gonna run in!"

I ran through the gate onto the field and shouted like an impression of a conquering hero.

"HEY GUYS, I CAN PLA . . .!"

I never finished my triumphant entrance, because I was stunned to see the pretty Catholic twins from my newspaper route talking to Charlie and John. What a stroke of luck I first thought. At last I had the chance to meet the two girls from my newspaper route, girls that I had been too bashful to speak with and I'd admired for so long – this was it!

"Hey, here comes Punchy," Charlie shouted.

My face reddened as I neared the twins and I did my best to pretend I hadn't heard Charlie's introduction. I wanted to crawl into a hole, when all my teammate echoed the shouts of "Hi Punchy," as if I was some kind of a clown.

John introduced me, "Beth and Mary, this is Punchy. He's our terrific Jew."

My spirits cringed with the words, "Punchy" and "Jew." I was introduced as a punch-drunk Jew to the Catholic twins that I'd been crazy to meet. I was too embarrassed to muster up anything but a weak smile and an even weaker greeting.

"Hi."

My two idols giggled, "Hello [giggle], Punchy."

It couldn't have been worse, because the pretty, dark hair twins seemed to be more amused than impressed by our meeting. Not only that, they didn't even recognize me as the newsboy, who delivered papers next door. I had always feared that I was invisible to them, now I was convinced. This wasn't going to be a good day unless I did something impressive on the football field.

Even though John had convinced shoeless Reds to join our 49ers team, I was told that the Baltimore Bears had recruited Buckie Brewster. Buckie was renowned in sandlot circles as the best straight ahead runner, but he was unique in his disdain for helmets. It's doubtful that a helmet was large enough to fit Buckie's enormous head and its thick mop of black hair.

Only about half of the players on the field were equipped in full football regalia, but except for Buckie, everyone wore some sort of helmet. Like Reds, who preferred to be shoeless, it seemed that Buckie preferred to be helmetless. He was our age, so Buckie couldn't be classified as a true ringer. Unfortunately, the Bears weren't ringer free.

John approached the Bears captain, punched his shoulder, and pointed to two tall blond guys on the Bears sideline. "Aren't they the McCoy brothers?"

"Uh . . . yeah, and we can't field a team without 'em."

"You gotta be kiddin me, they're seniors in high school. Damn . . . they gotta be at least three years older than any of us!"

"If you want to play this game, they gotta play. Anyway . . . you got Shoeless Reds."

"Get outta here! Reds is only fifteen - this is a rotten trick!"

John was furious, but he reluctantly agreed to let the McCoy brothers play, or there would be no game.

As the teams prepared for the game's start, I was determined to play well and make an impression on the pretty twins. Even with the McCoy brothers, by the second series of plays, it was clear that our two teams were evenly matched. Again and again, the Bears' helmet-less Buckie shed tacklers as he bulled through the middle of the 49ers line. Reds and I were able to bring Buckie down, but only after he made leg churning gains in yardage and a touchdown. On the other hand, shoeless Reds proved his worth to our team by spinning and scampering through the line and around the ends for big yardage and a tying score.

Near the end of the first half, the 49ers had the ball at mid-field, needing one yard for a first down. I had only carried the ball twice for short gains and was getting desperate to show my stuff in front of the twins.

"John, how-a-bout calling a play for me to carry the ball."

"Okay, dive play over center to Punch on two."

Our offense set up in the T formation, and I anxiously waited for the ball's snap, eager to crash through the line, side-step tacklers and dash for the goal line – the twins will love me.

"Hut one . . . Hut two!"

I cradled John's handoff with both hands, put my head down and drove into the hole off the center. It's as if the McCoy brothers had heard the play called in the huddle. They both met me head-on in the hole. My helmet plowed into one brother's chest, and it felt like I hit a brick wall, "OOF!" Then, I released a loud "OWW!" Because I had been stopped in my tracks, the other McCoy brother seized the opportunity to bend my head and neck, an abuse that caused additional pain. I crumpled to the turf in a painful heap with the oversized weight of the McCoy brothers on top of me.

Hearing my painful scream, John raced over to extricate me from the pile.

"Punch, are you Okay?"

"I don't think so." My neck throbbed with pain.

"What's the matter with your head? Can't you straighten your head out?" Harry screamed.

"What do you mean?"

"Damn! Your head's bent to one side!" John declared.

My neck hurt like the dickens. I hadn't realized that my head was cocked to one side, but my neck was in too much pain to bring my head upright.

"OWW, no I can't!"

"Jesus! Can't ya play?" Charlie asked.

It was evident to anyone with eyes and painfully obvious to me that I was done for the day.

"I'd better go home. It hurts too much and I can't straighten my head."

My teammates voiced their sympathy as I walked off, "Take it easy Punchy. I hope you'll be okay."

With my head bent to one side, I shuffled gingerly off the field. Even in this woeful state, I tried to look over to the twins. Only pity was on their pretty, Irish lassie faces. Pity was at least better than scorn, but I knew that any chance for a relationship with them was doomed forever. I had always dreamed of introducing myself to the twins after performing some heroic act, but those dreams were shattered the moment I had walked on and now limped off the field. Si stayed to watch the rest of the game while Billy walked with me on a slow and painful walk home.

Limping home, I was in too much pain to respond to my brother's repeated taunts.

"I told you, you'd be sorry."

Pop had to be at work and couldn't get over to see the game. If he had attended the game, I'm sure he would have immediately taken me to the emergency room. My brother was of no help to my wounded warrior's, mournful mood. I lost my chance with the twins, all three of my sandlot football games were incomplete, my neck was killing me, and I dreaded facing Mom with another injury without Pop's backing.

As soon as I entered the house and Mom saw my woebegone figure, she burst into tears.

"OY, VAI IZ MIR! YOUR HEAD and . . . what's happened to your NECK!?"

"I don't know, Mom. I was tackled and my neck got twisted."

"Can't you straighten your head?"

"No, it hurts like heck."

After a brief period of wailing and countless, "I told you, you would hurt yourself," Pop was summoned to take me to the emergency room.

On the way to the hospital, Pop didn't say a word. Whatever he was thinking, I knew it couldn't be good.

The emergency room was beginning to look too familiar to me, and the nurse at the desk recognized me. She pointed at me and laughed.

"You poor kid, are *you* back again?"

I was in no mood for humor and smiled wanly. After another long wait in a waiting room of misery and then being moved to another bright, white room, two male doctors arrived.

"How did this happen?" The intern asked.

"Football," I mumbled.

"Does it hurt?"

"You bet it does."

The older doctor offered a ray of hope that my pain would be relieved.

"Don't worry son, I think we can get you back to straight up and down."

He went to a glass door cabinet and pulled out a silver canister.

"This should do it."

As soon as the ice-cold liquid was sprayed on my neck, the two doctors worked together and slowly manipulated my head back to its natural, vertical position. It was a miracle, like the doctors had waved a magic wand. As soon as my head was perfectly straight, almost all of the pain in my neck disappeared.

"How do you feel?" The doctors asked.

Gingerly testing my head and neck movement, I was surprised to find that the sharp pain was gone.

"Gee, I don't believe it there's no pain. Thanks a lot."

Seeing me back to normal, Pop wiped his brow and let out a long sigh of relief.

Upon leaving the hospital, I was happy that my neck problem was solved, but I shuddered with the apprehension that storm clouds must be rising back at home. When Pop and I walked in the front door, there stood the matriarch, her hands on hips. An icy glare from her dark eyes caused me to feel flu-like shivers.

"WELL?" What did the doctor say?"

"Geordie's fine. The doctors straightened out his neck and he's just fine,"

"Kain einoreh! Fine you say! What next? Our son comes home from every game with one injury after another. Mein Got! Fine you say! Fun dayn moyl in gots oyers, from your mouth to God's ear."

"Gee Mom. I'm okay now – really!"

I moved my head from side to side to prove it didn't hurt. In fact, it hurt a little, but I didn't dare show it.

Tante Hinda, hearing the commotion, came down the stairs from her third floor apartment.

"Is Geordie all right?"

"It's none of your business," Pop shot back.

The hurt immediately appeared on my aunt's face. She stopped in the middle of the stairway, turned and walked wearily back up the steps to her apartment.

"That was terribly rude of you! "Why can't you be civil to my sister?"

"She should stay out of our affairs."

"She's family, she's concerned. What can be so wrong with that?"

Pop knew he'd better beat a retreat to his recliner – he was in trouble with Mom and that wasn't healthy. For the moment, concern for my injury was replaced by the father and sister-in-law dispute. There was no future in my sticking around, if the battle

140

should rage on. I crept up the stairs to the sanctity of the boys' bedroom.

A little later, Si returned home from the football game.

"We won!" Si exclaimed. "You shoulda seen the Bears' Buckie crash through our line. He put his head down, kept his legs going, and our guys just bounced off him. Thank goodness, we had Reds, and he was terrific. He ran great! They couldn't stop him. That guy, Buckie got a lot of yardage, but Reds scored the touchdowns that counted."

It was good to hear that the team won, but I lamented that my football experiences had been marred by fights, injuries, and Mom's disapproval. Even my long desire to meet the pretty Catholic twins had been dashed. My prestige and importance with the 49ers as their prime running back was being diminished by the addition of Reds, but I was even more determined to play with the 49ers.

"There's going to be another game with the Baltimore Bears next week."

"You're not gonna play again, are you?" Billy asked.

I grabbed my little brother and squeezed him in a bear hug.

"You bet I am!"

Si said in disbelief, "You're nuts!"

The Baltimore Bears and the 49ers faced off against each other once more. However, a surprising change in the lineup was announced. Buckie, the helmet-less running back for the same Baltimore Bears team had been recruited to play for the 49ers in our rematch. John was a great recruiter and there were no rules against stealing players from one team to the next. In fact, there were no rules – period. The Bears were openly upset that their star running back had been stolen, but they countered by enlisting my most hated opponent, McClaren.

McClaren snarled at me as we lined up for the opening kickoff, but I acted as if I didn't notice. John boomed the ball down the field. McClaren took the pigskin in the air, and galloped up the right sideline. I unleashed a flying tackle into the runner's mid-section and cracked McClaren out of bounds. The 49ers' players, who had feared that I might be timid after my injury, were relieved to see that their Punchy still had it in him.

"Way to go Punch!"

It was good to hear the praise, but I still hated hearing my despised nickname. Buckie and Reds were terrific running with the football. From the middle linebacker position, I made tackles from one side of the line to the other. We were too much for the Bears. McClaren couldn't get untracked and I was everywhere to stop him. The few times that I ran the ball I was able to make good gains. On the opening play of the second half, I dashed off tackle, into McClaren's arms, but before he could bring me down, I spun out of the tackler's arms and ran free for a touchdown.

"Where'd you learn a move like that?" Buckie, who was strictly a straight ahead runner, asked while greeting me in the end zone.

"I don't know, I just did it," I answered matter-of-factly.

The game became a rout, while my self-confidence soared with every tackle and successful running play. The rest of the game was all 49ers – we won 35-0. McClaren stomped off the field the moment the game's end was announced by the timekeeper, someone fortunate enough to own a watch. The 49ers were thrilled that they were undefeated, but didn't realize that this game would be their last of the season. With the addition of shoeless Reds and no-helmet Buckie, our team had become too strong and no other neighborhood team dared play us.

After two weeks without opponents, John realized there would be no other games to be played, and he organized a celebratory march. I joined the team in a procession up and down the neighborhood streets. We shouted to no one in particular, extolling our undefeated record. Even though I felt that much of our record was tainted, I marched and shouted like everyone else.

"WE'RE THE 49ers! WE'RE NUMBER ONE!
WE'RE UNDEFEATED!"

Fortunately, none of the parade's viewers interrupted our celebration to ask, "Who won the radios in the raffle?" The whereabouts of Morrie was still unknown, but it was generally believed that Morrie had been caught shoplifting and was most likely in some place of detention designed for larcenous kids. Since the result of the raffle drawing hadn't become an issue, Morrie and the radios were soon forgotten. After the celebration, John, the 49ers and I went our separate neighborhood ways, reopening the social chasm between us.

CHAPTER TWENTY-ONE
RED BELLY

Over the winter, snow balling the trolleys on Spruce Street wasn't much fun anymore. After one bad particularly bad experience, we decided to declare a truce and forgo the fun we once had in pelting the trolleys.

Our one bad experience occurred onn one snowy evening in December. Don, Si and I had set up our trolley ambush position near the 44th Street corner's position and amassed an arsenal of snowballs. We crouched behind a bush at the sight of the Number 42 trolley descending the hill from 45th Street. Our first victim for the night made its stop at the 44th Street corner, picked up a passenger, and started to move down the Spruce Street hill. The three of us stood up from our hiding place and began to gleefully bombard the trolley. Our snowballs were direct hits that burst magnificently against the trolley's windows. We took great delight in seeing the passengers cringe at the sound of the snowballs smacking against the trolley's windows.

Si cheered, "This is great!"

Don said, "Oh, Oh . . . The trolley's stopped! Why did it stop?"

The trolley had come to an abrupt stop. Snowballed trolleys had never stopped before. Not only did the trolley stop, but we were shocked to see the door open and the conductor bound out onto the street.

"OH, OH . . . HE'S COMING AFTER US!"

This was the very first time that a conductor had exited the trolley, and we weren't sure what to do. This trolley's conductor had enough of these attacks. He was sick and tired of his trolley being hit by snowballs. We were probably not his only assailants on his run that night, and he decided he wasn't going to take it anymore. We went into full retreat mode and began to run up 44th Street past Don's house, but the pavement was covered with three inches of snow and slowed our escape. Don looked back over his shoulder and saw that the conductor was catching up.

"RUN FASTER [wheeze] HE'S GAINING ON US!"

For an old man, the trolley guy was in pretty good shape, but the slippery sidewalk did him in. Halfway up the block the driver hit an especially slick patch. His legs went up, his head lurched back, and the conductor performed a half gainer with a backward twist into a snow bank. In gymnastics or diving, he would have received high marks.

Don looked back again and caught a glimpse of the record breaking fall by a trolley conductor.

"HE'S DOWN!"

That became our last trolley snowballing experience. The trolley driver had violated the unwritten rules of trolley snowballing. We're supposed to pelt the trolley and the trolley was obligated to absorb the snowball assault and keep on going. It wasn't fun anymore – we retired.

In the beginning of the summer, I arrived home to give my family news about my new job. I found my brother Si talking on the telephone and stopped to listen to his side of the conversation:

"Yes Maam, five dollars for every cat."

"Like I said, I'm calling from the University of Pennsylvania's Veterinary School. We need of as many cats as we can get."

"Uh, uh."

"Do you have a cat?"

"I see. Do you know where you can get cats? That's fine. Bring them down to the veterinary school on 37th and Baltimore Avenue. We'll take all the cats you can bring us."

Holding the phone in one hand and his hand over his mouth with the other, Si tried to stifle his laughter.

"Will we take good care of the cats? We certainly will and thank you."

The moment Si set down the phone, he exploded with laughter.

"Si, what in the heck is that all about? What's so funny?"

"I'm just having some fun with dumb people."

"You know, you could get in trouble doing that."

"How would anyone know? Anyway . . . it's fun."

"Okay, but I got news for you. I won't be delivering newspapers anymore."

"How come, you won't?"

"I've got a Branch Captain's job like Wolfie around 36th and Powelton."

"I thought you were nuts playing football with those Ludlow guys, but now I know you've completely lost it. That's a really rough neighborhood – you'll be killed."

"It's a lot more money than delivering papers and I need the money for college."

I had been reluctant to take the job, because of the area's reputation for crime and poverty. The area was mostly made up of poor whites and even poorer Negroes. The job turned out to be a character builder for me. I had to deal with newsboys that would do their darnedest to cheat me, if they could. I was warned that the newsboys would steal newspapers, shortchange me, or disappear with their weekly collections.

I wised up to one little trick where I'd be handed a stack of dollar bills and one or more of the bills had been folded in half to make a single bill counted twice. As a Branch Captain, I learned not to trust anyone. I couldn't be a Wolfie, but I began to understand what might have made him a Nazi tyrant.

I got a first-hand look at squalor, poverty, and crime. On one day, I was forced to go out on a missing carrier's route to make his weekly collections. One of the carrier's customers was on the second floor of a dilapidated apartment building. In a creepy, dark hallway, I knocked on the door. I waited . . . and waited, but I heard nothing. After another minute or two I detected the sound of muffled voices, chairs squeaking across a wooden floor, and rustling of paper. I waited . . . and waited. Finally, the door opened a crack and I got a glimpse of a black face. In a deep, gruff voice, the face said, "Whatcha want boy?"

"I'm collecting for the Bulletin."

"How much is it kid?"

"It's $1.70 for two weeks."

The door opened a little wider to a brightly lit room. I got a glimpse of lots of money, piles of coins and bills on a table in the middle of the room. It must have been the headquarters for a numbers racket. A couple of mean looking, black men were seated at the table and turned to scowl at me that sent shivers down my spine. It was a warm day, the hallway was musty and close, and nervous sweat began to exude from my every pore of my body. Suddenly, a hand appeared around the door's edge and dumped two crumpled dollar bills in my outstretched hand.

"Keep the change kid. Now . . . get your little white ass the hell outta here!"

I didn't need his invitation. I bolted down the hallway and hopped down the stairway, three steps at a time. Days like that made me hate the Branch Captain's job, but I held the job for the entire summer and took a second job with the Model laundry around the corner on Locust Street.

Before the summer hiatus ended, "Red Belly" initiations had been introduced in the neighborhood. The "Red Belly" was dreamed up by a bunch of bored, overly aggressive Ludlow Street guys, mostly by my 49ers' teammates. They had nothing better to do than harass each other and everyone else. Willing and unwilling male individuals, from ages eight to sixteen, were grabbed by a roving mob and pinned to the ground. The victims' shirts were pulled up to bare their bellies, and the bellies were slapped until the skin blossomed into a beautiful crimson shade.

The whacking was painful and the sting from the inflamed belly lasted long after the attack. It was believed to be some sort

147

of a rite of passage. Considering some African tribal rites of passage, like hunting lions with a spear or walking on red hot coals, the Red Belly wasn't that bad.

My brothers and all my friends had received the Red Belly, everyone except me. Because I spent most of my daylight hours working at the newspaper branch or shaking damp clothing at the Model laundry while listening to the hilarious radio comic team of Bob Elliot and Ray Gould, I had avoided the Red Belly attacks. This was a fact that hadn't gone unnoticed by John and the rest of the Ludlow Gang. With the summer almost over, John and his Red Belly, assault battalion concluded it was about time to "Get Punchy." On a Sunday afternoon, an enthusiastic Red Belly posse, led by John, was formed for their march down 44th Street, intent on initiating me.

Unaware of the approaching mob, I sat on the front porch with Mom while reading Life magazine. She was busy finishing off the Bulletin's crossword puzzle. My mother's linguistic skills and knowledge of literature and ancient history enabled her to dust off a crossword puzzle in record time. I was surprised to hear a groan and a sigh come from my mother. I looked up from my magazine to see her put the newspaper down, look at the back of her hands and tears welled up in her eyes.

"Mom, you're not crying are you?"

"Geordie, look at my hands . . . will you. I used to have such beautiful hands. Now, they're wrinkled and old looking from doing the laundry and washing dishes."

Before I could think of something to say to soothe my mother's feelings I noticed Jeff's ears begin to perk up. My concern for my mother was diverted for the moment. Jeff perked up and stuck his nose through the porch railing's posts. At that point, I heard the sound of many footsteps and voices coming from the approaching Red Belly mob.

Jumping up from the rocking chair, I leaned over the porch's railing and peered down the street. I immediately recognized the crowd of a dozen or so led by John and a number of my 49ers' teammates. There was no doubt in my mind that they were coming to initiate me. I had heard rumors floating in the neighborhood that indicated I was due for the Red Belly initiation. The gang came up to the front steps in great spirits. They were laughing and joking and relishing their plan to "Get Punchy."

When the mob reached our porch, John announced from the pavement, "Punchy, we're here to give you a Red Belly-we don't want no trouble."

My mother rose out of her chair and cried out to me. "Geordie, what are they saying, Punchy and Red Belly?"

Red Belly was one thing that I could brush off, but to call me Punchy in front of my mother created in me a volatile combination of embarrassment and anger. Jeez, why did they have to call me Punchy in front of my mother?

"Forget it guys! No chance! No dice!"

"You boys, GO AWAY!" My mother shouted.

"Mom, don't worry, I can handle this myself." I strode deliberately to the top of the porch steps. "Get outta here you guys!"

John shouted, "We'll see about that. C'mon gang, let's get 'im!"

Ignoring my mother's protests, John, Charlie, and Harry led the charge up the concrete-slab porch steps. I held my position at the top of the steps, and the three leaders laughed their fool heads off while they grabbed my arms to haul me off the porch, but I wasn't about to be embarrassed in front of my mother.

Overcome by an irrational rage of resistance, I struggled as hard as I could, but they held me too tight to pull away and tried to drag me down the steps. Reminiscent of my decision to leap off the garage roof, without further thought or hesitation, I bent my knees and propelled myself off the porch in an injury-be-damned, headlong leap. Charlie, John, and Harry were too surprised to release their grip on my arms and involuntarily joined me in the flight off the porch.

Our hurtling bodies crashed into surprised victims standing on the steps, and like an avalanche we gathered more and more bodies down with us. The avalanche of bodies landed in a heap on top of the poor devils standing at the bottom of the steps. Cries of agony arose from the pile of twisted and crushed bodies. The most unfortunate were the ones that ended on the bottom of the pile and bore the brunt of the fall onto the unforgiving, concrete pavement. Their pain was exacerbated by the weight of the bodies that plummeted upon them.

I had landed unscathed on top of the pile of pained humanity and managed to extricate myself from the assorted, contorted torsos and limbs. With utter disdain, I stood over the bodies for a moment and strutted back up the steps onto the porch.

One by one, each of the would-be attackers slowly, painfully got to their feet, checked for broken bones, and looked up at me in a mixture of anger, frustration and disbelief. Fortunately, no one was seriously damaged.

When John removed himself from the pile of bodies, he bent over and rubbed his throbbing back and roared, "JESUS CHRIST! Punch, what in the *hell* did you do that for? ARE YOU CRAZY? You coulda killed someone. Everyone else has gotten a Red Belly, WHY NOT YOU?"

"I jumped accidentally on purpose. Anyway . . . just because everyone else is nuts doesn't mean I gotta go along with something as stupid as a Red Belly."

The gang gathered up their wounded, all the while cursing and growling obscenities at me. John and his cohorts milled around at the bottom of the steps for several minutes and discussed the possibility of another assault.

John declared, "Like hell I'm not going up after him again! Punchy's nuts! Christ, you don't know what he'll do next! We might as well head home–HE'S A LOUSY SPORT!"

The shout of "lousy sport" was for my benefit, but I couldn't care less. The Red Belly posse stood around for a few minutes longer, glaring up at me and grousing all the time. Finally, they began to trudge back down the street. This was a far cry from the exuberant crowd that had come to "Get Punchy."

I stood triumphantly at the porch's railing and watched my attackers disappear down the street. I turned to sit down and saw the weirdest look on my mother's face– she couldn't believe what she just saw. Flopping in my chair, I couldn't conceal a smile of extreme satisfaction. In the remaining days of summer, there were no further attempts to apply the *Red Belly* to me.

When John was later asked, "What're we gonna do about Punchy?"
"Nuttin. You can't tell what that crazy bastard will do."

I was just as surprised as John at what I had done. I realized that my leap off the porch was as reckless as the leap from the garage roof, but I was pretty sure that I wasn't crazy. Success in football may have given me the self-confidence that wouldn't let me be humiliated in front of my mother, but feelings of regret still lingered for failing to help Pop face up to Ricky and Mickey or not standing by Mom's side against the mob that had come to get Pop and me. Now, I felt somewhat vindicated over that shame I had harbored for so long. Even the surprised, but satisfied expression on my mother's face meant a lot to me.

Later that day, when Pop heard Mom's recount of the Red Belly incident, he understood that she was torn between a sense of a pride in the way her son resisted the mob, but was more concerned over his rashness.
"I tell you, he was meshugeh in leaping off the porch like that – he could have killed himself. It's a miracle that he didn't break something."
"Was anyone hurt?"

"One of those ruffians do you mean? No, but it would have been good riddance to bad rubbish."

Pop laughed and said, "I'm glad no one was hurt, but it sounds to me that our son has become a man. Even though, he may be a bit meshugeh."

CHAPTER TWENTY-TWO
A 49er AGAIN

As my Junior Year at West Philadelphia High began, I hadn't expected to play sandlot football with the 49ers, especially after I frustrated the gang's attempt to Red Belly me. I was certain that they were royally pissed at me, and I didn't have too many kind thoughts about them.

But on a Saturday afternoon early in September, these unkind thoughts were quickly dispelled, when Harry cruised up to the deli steps where my brothers and I were lounging and lunching on Sam's tasty hoagies.

"How are you doing, Geordie?"

"Oh . . . Harry . . . what's up?"

"Geordie, I know you're pissed at the guys, but we need you on our team. We've got a game in a couple-a weeks with a really good team."

"What the heck . . . ever since they tried to Red Belly me, I haven't even seen any of those guys!"

"Listen . . . you gotta know ya coulda killed somebody, but . . . hey, all is forgotten."

"Oh yeah, I haven't forgotten."

"Listen, we need you. You're still our best tackler. Reds and Buckie are back on the team, but you're our best linebacker and still as good a running back as them."

Listening to Harry's coaxing, Si' face reddened and he snarled, "Damn Geordie, you'll get beat up just like last year."

Billy chimed in, "Mom sure as heck won't let you play again with those guys."

Harry fumed, "How-about you two clamming up–I ain't talking to you–I'm talking to your brother! Anyway, we're gonna have full football equipment this year for the whole team, so he won't get hurt."

153

"Full equipment . . . HA that's rich!" Billy scoffed. "How's equipment gonna stop Geordie from getting knifed or his head bent out of shape?"

"Anyway, where do you think you're getting the equipment?" Si sneered.

"We're gonna raffle off a television this year."

Si rolled his eyes and stuck out his chin at Harry.

"How's Morrie gonna steal it for you? I hear he's still in prison!"

"Hell no, no one's seen Morrie for a year! We're gonna raise enough money in a raffle to buy the TV prize and the equipment we need."

"Yeah, just like you got the radios," Billy snickered.

"Listen, you little pip squeak Gadget, zip it or I'll zip it for you," Harry said, shaking his fist in Billy's face.

Too deep in thought to pay attention to the banter between my brothers and Harry, my mind raced over last year's football experience. I recalled the fun I had, but winced in thinking about the fights and injuries. I concluded that tackles and touchdowns won out over all the other stuff.

"Okay Harry, but things must be different this year. I like football and would like to play, but not mess with all that other crap."

That's all Harry wanted to hear–he jumped in the air and thrust his fist in the air.

"Ya mean you'll play?"

"Yeah, I'll play."

"That's great! When I tell John, he'll be as happy as hell."

Harry left our Deli group shouting and bouncing.

The very next day, across the street from the high school, another unexpected football opportunity arose. After school, I had a nickel to burn to buy a pretzel at the soft pretzel vendor's stand. Only a Philadelphian can truly appreciate the city's renowned soft pretzel. My mouth watered over the delectable pretzel, sprinkled with good old Philly grime, slopped on with a watery, yellowish,

154

mustard tasting substance. Just as I was about to take a bite of my prized pretzel, I heard someone calling my name. Looking up from the pretzel, I saw my brother, Si, racing in my direction from across the street. Si reached me out of breath.

"Can I . . . [pant] . . . have a bite?"

"Is that why you came running and shouting? No, you can't take a bite."

"Be that way, but I'm glad I found you. Guys told me they're looking for more football players on West Philly's football team. Guys that know you say you're as good as lots of them on the team."

"Gee, Si . . . I . . . I'm not sure."

"It's a lot better than getting your head beat in playing with those Ludlow guys."

"They say I'm good enough to be on the high school team?"

"Yep, they know you."

"Well, if whoever they are . . . think I'm good enough, maybe I should at least give it a shot!"

I celebrated my decision to play football for the West Philly High team by polishing off my Philadelphia soft pretzel, mustard looking substance, grime, and all. I smiled to Si and said, "West Philadelphia High football, here I come!"

The first day at high school practice I faced immediate disillusionment. At 5'9" and 150 pounds and dressed in an ill-fitting practice-uniform, I didn't exactly fit the picture of a football player that would impress a coach. Needless to say, I failed to impress. My pants were baggy, shoes were too large, and the white leather helmet was at least a size too big. Without an opportunity for the coach to see me run, catch or tackle, I was immediately relegated to the Junior Varsity. My size and sloppy appearance made me invisible to the JV coach. I wasn't given a look or an opportunity to play a down in the daily JV scrimmages.

Meanwhile, for the next two weeks, the 49ers' team fanned out throughout the neighborhood to sell raffle tickets for a television prize. The raffle tickets' price was higher, which made sales harder to come by. This year's sandlot team had three unique, but good running backs: Buckie still without a helmet, Reds without shoes, and "Punchy" me. Team practices were held on the Sanatorium's field. By now, players were better equipped and practices were better organized. A defensive formation and a few basic offensive plays had been devised, which made us seem more like a real football team.

Only days before the season's first sandlot game, John expressed his worry at a team practice that raffle sales were far short of our needs, "C'mon you guys, we gotta sell more tickets. I think we've got enough money for the equipment we need, but so far, there's not enough for the TV prize."

We hit the streets again, harassed our parents, relatives, friends, neighbors, shoppers, everyone and anyone to buy raffle tickets. Stopping short of muggings, we were as aggressive in our sales approach as legally possible.

By game day, the team gathered in front of John's house on Ludlow Street and our team captain proudly pointed to a pile of shoulder and hip pads, pants, helmets, and other football paraphernalia.

I said, "Gee John – that's great. I sure can use pants and pads. I guess raffle sales were good."

"They coulda been better."

"Who won the television?" Harry asked.

"Someone, that's who."

"Someone?"

"Look fellas, I guess I better be straight with you. There's no TV, 'cause we didn't sell enough tickets to buy the TV and the equipment. Keep your lips zipped about it."

In retrospect, it might have been better, and a lot more honest, if the team had forgotten the bogus raffle concept and simply tried to solicit money to support the team. The TV raffle began as an honest effort, but it just didn't work out that way

Game day arrived. What a difference there was in seeing that all the 49ers'players, as well as their opponents, almost fully outfitted in football gear. The game was played on a lined, regulation football field with goal posts, and we were assured that we wouldn't be chased in the middle of the game. The timekeeper was still someone with a watch, who kept a running clock and the referees were a couple of so-called disinterested observers. In any case, the game sized up to be more like a real football game than anything our team had played thus far.

The ensuing play between the 49ers and the Hornets was rough but legal. There were no unkind references to parental lineage or sucker punches, just hard blocking, tackling and running. Shoeless Reds was still shoeless and Buckie still declined the protection of a helmet, but the two were good football players and ran and tackled well. Reds scampered through the line and around the ends for long runs while would-be tacklers grabbed air. Buckie made big gains with bull-like rushes with legs churning and shedding tacklers as he gobbled up yardage. I pitched in with a couple of good runs for first downs, but we managed to score only a single touchdown, in spite of the positive yardage accumulated by our backs. Just before half-time Buckie scored with a short dive into the end zone and John kicked the extra point.

At middle linebacker, I had gained confidence and tried to improve my tackling by using shoulders instead of helmet butts in my tackles. I made crushing tackles, play after play, in punishing the Hornets' backs. In the third quarter, the Hornets quarterback was effective by avoiding the 49ers' linemen's rushes and gave our defensive backs' fits. In two drives, he launched two perfectly thrown, long passes to his receivers in full stride. Both passes went for touchdowns, but the two extra-point kicks went wide of the goalposts.

It was a frustrating game for our team. We had piled up good yardage on offense, but each time we failed to make a crucial play in third down situations. The running clock was running down and only minutes remained in the game. We had driven the ball down to the Hornets twenty yard line, trailing 12-7, when Buckie fumbled the ball to the Hornets at the line of scrimmage.

The guy with the watch, the official timekeeper, shouted out the seriousness of our game situation.

"Only two minutes to go!"

It was desperation time, and it looked like we had officially lost our first game. Instead of sitting on the ball and running out the clock, the cocky Hornets team chose to rub it in and run a play. Seeing the Hornet's back sweep around right end with two blockers in front of him, I pursued along the line of scrimmage and knifed in between two blockers to intercept the running back. Still unable to completely break the habit of using my helmet in tackling, I drove my helmet directly into the ball.

"OOF!"

The surprised ball carrier coughed up the football.

"FUMBLE!"

Noticing the ball squirt from the runner's grasp, I pivoted after the loose ball and pounced on the fumble.

"IT'S OUR BALL!"

There was no time to celebrate.

John shouted, "No time – Huddle up!"

"Thirty seconds," the timekeeper hollered.

John exhorted the team in the huddle, "Harry, cut to the left corner of the end zone. You guys gotta give me time to throw.

"Block you guys – BLOCK- on one!"

The 49ers' team broke the huddle and ran to line up over the ball. If the ball could be put in play before the timekeeper's watch ran out, this would surely be the last play of the game.

John barked, "Down, Set, Hut One!"

Taking the center snap, John faded back as the two lines collided. Harry ran straight to the end zone and cut left to the far corner. Harry's sharp move left the defensive back scrambling to

158

stay with him. The Hornets middle linebacker hurdled Reds' diving block, and lunged at our quarterback. John sidestepped the rusher and lofted a tight spiral that spun in a perfect arc toward the end zone. Harry sighted the ball's trajectory and raced desperately to reach the back corner of the end zone. Just as the football descended into the corner, Harry lunged and stretched to his fullest. As he flattened out on the turf, the ball fell into his hands for a touchdown.

"TOUCHDOWN," the 49ers and supporters shouted.

The entire 49ers team and all of our supporters went nuts and raced into the end zone to bury Harry. The stunned Hornets fell to their knees and beat the ground with their fists.

Arguments erupted from the Hornets fans, insisting that the clock must have run out.

"NO TOUCHDOWN! The clock ran out!"

The 49ers' backers shouted the protestors down.

"TOUCHDOWN! The play had already started before the clock ran out!"

Both teams ignored the arguments and walked off the field. The 49ers knew they had won and laughed and cheered as they strutted victoriously on their way, across the field to the old Packard. The Hornets team couldn't believe they lost, but were too shocked to join in their fans' complaints.

The ride home in the old Packard was a joyous one. I was heaped with praise for my game saving tackle and fumble recovery. John and Harry were hailed as heroes as we rehashed the game.

"WHAT A PASS AND CATCH!" Smitty crowed.

Loud cheers arose from a team that registered one of its few legitimate victories. A few groans were audible coming from those in the most cramped conditions. In driving the jammed Packard home with a gang of noisy, young football players, Pop seemed to enjoy the victory almost as much as his passengers.

The fact that I played well made the win that much sweeter for my father. When Pop got his first good look at me seated beside him, he winced to see my cut lip, skinned nose, and a trickle of dried blood that oozed from my battered nose. Even in college and professional football, only a few linemen wore face guards, and even fewer backs wore a single bar mounted on their helmets. Without face protection, my face continued to absorb a beating in games and practices.

It didn't take long for Mom to notice my battered face, the moment my father and I entered the vestibule.

"Oy, *Vai iz mir! Not again! Look at you!"* Mom threw her hands to her face.

My face looked worse than it really was, but it only added fuel to the fire of her resistance to my playing football, especially with "those hooligans."

Pop put his arm around Mom's shoulder, and in soothing tones attempted to calm his distraught wife, "Now, now Fannie. . . it's just a few scrapes. He's had a lot worse than that."

"Lord love a duck . . . that's supposed to make me feel better!"

Pop realized that nothing he would say could possibly soothe Mom's feelings about football, and he headed directly for refuge in his living room recliner.

The dinner table that evening was unusually quiet. I felt my mother's disapproving looks, and tried to eat my dinner while covering my face with one hand and slumping down over the dinner plate. Every so often Mom would turn to catch sight of my marred face, wince, and sorrowfully shake her head, while Pop just tried not to look at me. My brothers and sisters snickered from time to time, only to be silenced by Mom's icy glare.

Helen tried to break the tension with news, "Mom and Pop, did you see that the Pines got a new car?"

Dad said, "The ghost business must be good and now, they're living the Life of Riley."

Mom's face curled up in disgust and said, "They're still a disgrace to the neighborhood. They still dress their children in shmattehs, and there's trash on their porch and in their backyard."

160

"Gee, Fannie, whenever I see Mister and Missus Pine, they always speak well of you."

My father's attempt at humor was received by my mother's pillar-of-salt-look - straight out of the Old Testament.

CHAPTER TWENTY-THREE
THE CHEERLEADERS

Still aching from the battering that I took in the Hornets game, I didn't feel much like going to Monday's JV football practice. What was the use? I had gone to every practice for two weeks and the coach hadn't given me so much as a look on offense or defense. But this day was different. For the first time, the JV coach took notice of the kid in the sloppy, ill-fitting uniform. What was different about me? The uniform still looked ludicrous on me and my feet would never grow into those floppy cleats. What was it? It was my scraped up and battered face – that was it.

"What in the hell happened to . . . uh? What's your name kid?

"Geordie Eaton . . . coach."

"Eaton is it? You look like you were in a fight and lost?"

"I got these scrapes playing in my team's football game yesterday."

"Playing football?"

"Yeah, I play for the 49ers, and we beat the Hornets yesterday."

"Don't you know you're not allowed to play football outside, when you play high school football?

"Nope, but I'm sorry coach. I didn't think it'd matter anyway, since I haven't played any here."

"Hmmm - what position do you play?"

"I play halfback on offense and middle linebacker on defense."

Suddenly, the coach took interest in the shlumpy looking kid that he had discounted as a player the moment he saw him. Because the JV coach wasn't completely satisfied with his team and the fact that I actually played on some kind of a football team, he decided to give me a chance to play in the day's scrimmage against Overbrook High.

Half way through the scrimmage, I heard the coach shout, "Eaton, get in there at middle linebacker."

If I could have done cartwheels, I would have. I dashed on the field. On the very first defensive play, Overbrook's quarterback threw a quick jump pass over the middle to the crossing wingback. The instant the ball reached the receiver, I drove my shoulder into the receiver's back and the ball was jarred loose, falling harmlessly to the turf. Not only was the coach impressed with the force of the tackle, but my quick reaction to the play showed good football instincts. After a number of aggressive tackles on defense, the coach decided to give me a shot on offense.

"Now, let's see what you can do running the ball. Go in at Fullback . . . right formation . . . Fullback . . . Two hole dive . . . On three . . . Break!"

West Philly lined up in its single wing formation. Receiving the direct snap from the Center, I took one step toward the Number Two hole, but I saw see there was no hole and decided to head for daylight around right end. The defensive end had gone for my move toward the line and was easily blocked to the inside by our wingback. Breaking free around end, I gained more than ten yards before being dragged down by two tacklers.

Returning sheepishly to the huddle, I was concerned that I'd get a scolding for not following the coach's call.

"I'm sorry coach. I tried to run the two-hole, but it was closed, so I just tried to get as much yardage as I could."

Amused by my apology and thoroughly impressed by my creative move, all the coach could do was chuckle.

"That's okay Eaton. I can't teach what you just did."

I played the rest of the scrimmage at linebacker and fullback, and the coach was impressed that he had found a good linebacker and a natural running back.

That evening, at the dinner table, I broke the news to the family.

"I played real well today in our Overbrook scrimmage. The coach really liked the way I played.

"That's good son," Pop said, smiling proudly.

"He told me that I can't play with the 49ers anymore."

"Mazltov! That's the best news yet!" Mom declared and couldn't be happier. "God has answered my prayers. You won't be playing with those ruffians anymore."

A few days later, John and Harry met me at Sam's. They had come to get me to play in a rematch with the Hornets team.

"Geordie we need you this Saturday. Those Hornets guys claimed they were cheated by our last second touchdown."

"I'm sorry, guys. I'd like to play, but I can't – it's against the high school football rules."

Harry was dejected, "Yeah, yeah, I thought I heard somethin' 'bout that."

John, "Look Punchy, we really need ya, but you're too good to mess around in sandlot football, especially if you can play in high school. You're doin' the right thing."

It was then that I realized that John, with all his macho bluster, had grown to appreciate me and was genuinely happy to see me succeed at a higher level. I felt good in that realization, and gave Harry and John a parting punch to their shoulders as they turned to go.

"Thanks guys. I'll see you around and good luck."

I looked after them as they disappeared around the 44th Street corner. My final thought was that I appreciated John's good wishes, but I wouldn't miss being called Punchy.

It was halfway through the football season and my play on the JV team got me moved up to the varsity. The JV coach hated to lose me, but he was my biggest booster to the varsity coaches. I played sparingly as a backup to a tall, rangy middle linebacker. When I had the opportunity to play in varsity games, I played well enough to impress the varsity coaches with my tackling and running ability. West Philly High ended the season with more wins than losses, and the prospects for next season were even better.

Playing high school football gave me great satisfaction that I finally had the opportunity to play in a football game on a regulation field, football officials, stands filled with cheering fans, bands belting out high school fight songs, and pretty cheerleaders dancing and hollering through megaphones. This was the real football that I had longed to play.

On my way home after school, I was hailed and stopped by two tall, willowy, pretty girls. With the prettiest smiles, they said in unison, "Can we have your autograph?"

The football season was over, but I recognized the two as cheerleaders. I didn't have any classes with them and it never crossed my mind that I'd have the chance to meet them. My first instinct was the two girls were putting me on.

"Are you kidding me?"

"Sorta," the blond responded, "I'm Mary."

"We've wanted to meetcha" the brunette added, "I'm Jessica."

"I'll bite, why did you want to meet me?"

Mary said, "We're cheerleaders and we've been cheering for the team and you the whole season. Honestly, we think you're cute."

"Yeah, sure . . . now I know you're kiddin' me."

Jessica said, "No, we're not . . . really. How about walking us home?"

"I'd like to, but I gotta get to work right now."

Jessica smiled the sweetest smile I'd ever seen.

"We live in the apartment houses on Chestnut Street. Why don't you bring a friend and come over on Saturday afternoon, around one.

"Yeah . . . eh . . . okay . . . sounds great."

"We'll be waiting outside on the front steps."

"Yep, I'll be seeing you Saturday."

"Are you sure?"

"Sure!"

"We'll be waiting."

Heading for my job at the laundry, I glorified in the thought that things were looking up for me, girl-wise. Two gorgeous cheerleaders seem to think of me as some kind of football hero. Football was beginning to have a few real perks, so I thought. Even though Don was my best friend, I decided to ask Bob to join me to meet the cheerleaders. I felt that Bob was smoother with girls and I needed all the help I could get.

"Well, whatcha say?"

Bob didn't need any coaxing, "Hot damn! You bet I will. Thanks for asking me pal – I'm hot to trot!"

On Saturday, Bob and I set out for our meeting with the cheerleaders. I couldn't believe my good fortune, and Bob was salivating just thinking about it. When we rounded the corner onto Chestnut Street, I spotted the two girls sitting on the stone steps of the apartment building.

"There they are, Bob. Aren't they pretty?"

Bob nodded, "Yep, they look real good to me already."

"Wait until you see them up close – they're knockouts!"

After we joined the cheerleaders and exchanged friendly introductions, it appeared that our foursome was hitting it off. That is until I noticed Mary's smile transform into a frown. Her gaze was fixed past me to something further down Chestnut Street. I turned to see what had caught Mary's attention. She had spotted John leading a band of about six 49ers' players up the street toward us. As John's entourage got closer, I could see by their stride and the look on their faces that this wouldn't be a pleasant encounter.

When John and his group reached us, John spit out, "What's up Punchy? What in the hell are you doing with our girls? You don't even play with us anymore, and now you come into our neighborhood and try to take over."

"Hey John, what do you mean by *your* neighborhood? This isn't Ludlow Street. For crying out loud, I just met them, and I didn't know they were *your* girls. Hell, anyway, they're the ones that should decide who they belong to, if anyone!"

John groused, "Bullshit!"

I looked to Mary and Jessica for support. Mary held her palms up with her head to one side and Jessica looked away. Apparently the girls were too intimidated by John and not about to stand up for themselves.

I asked, "Well . . . what do you say, Mary?" No answer. "Jessica?" She fidgeted and looked away again.

I knew that Bob wouldn't be of much help, if things got physical–Bob was a lover, not a fighter. Seeing that the cheerleaders and Bob gave me no choice, I shrugged my shoulders and faced John.

"I guess . . . that's it John. I really wasn't trying to steal *your* girlfriends, but from this point on, you and I have nuthin' more to say to each other."

"Hey Punchy, ya shouldn't feel that way–just don't think you can come into our neighborhood and take our girls."

My voice dropped a couple of octaves, "You and the 49ers can kiss my ass, and by the way, don't ever call me Punchy again. I hated that name, and now . . . I don't have to take that crap from you or the rest of you crumb bums."

I turned on my heels and stomped away. Bob, who had been harboring thoughts of a full-scale retreat, wiped the sweat off his brow and hustled to catch up to me.

John and his group stared open mouthed at my grand exit, and the girls stared at their shoes.

John called out, "Geez Punchy, don't go away mad."

Without looking back, not breaking stride, my middle finger was thrust straight up so it couldn't be missed.

Bob had to break into a trot to catch up with me.

"I guess that's it for the cheerleaders, huh?"

"Yeah, Bob, that's it for the cheerleaders and those bums too."

CHAPTER TWENTY-FOUR
REVENGE

Being recognized as an athlete, a football player might have advantages with admiration from some girls in school, but it had disadvantages as well. Some of my teachers seemed to look at athletes as dumb and unworthy of their time and effort.

My first stab at Geometry was frustrated by a hatchet-faced witch of a teacher, who couldn't care less that I wasn't keeping up with the angles, axioms and theorems. Since I was a football player, she assumed that I must be stupid and I was relegated to a desk in the back of the geometry classroom. I didn't keep up with the class and I failed geometry, which was the first time I ever failed or even came close to failing a course.

Even my history teacher assumed the worst of me and attempted to embarrass the only football player in class, me.

He used me as a guinea pig in his lesson on the conflict between the British and the Spanish Armada on July 29, 1588. "Even though the British fleet was outnumbered by the Armada, the British fleet had longer range guns than the Spanish Armada's ships. I'll demonstrate with someone in the class . . . Eaton come up here."

Unsure of what my teacher had in mind, I joined him to face my tittering classmates.

"Simply by staying out of range of the Spaniards' guns, the British fleet, armed with longer range cannons, was able to rain tremendous fire power on the Spanish ships. Let me demonstrate. Now, Mister Eaton, I'll represent a British ship that had the longer range guns and you will be a Spanish ship that had the shorter range guns." The history teacher stretched out one arm and clamped his hand down firmly on my shoulder. "Now . . .

you'll be a Spanish ship that had smaller-range guns, and I want you to try to place your hand on my shoulder."

Because the history teacher was about three inches taller, he fully expected that my hand couldn't reach his shoulder. He didn't realize that I had unusually long arms for my height. To his sputtering surprise and the raucous amusement of the class, I stretched my arm out and placed my hand squarely on the teacher's shoulder. Because of the failed experiment, I found that I became an enemy to my history teacher and I had to work extra hard, just to get a decent grade.

Not all my scholastic problems could be attributed to teachers' bias against athletes. In a family that academic excellence was expected, it was difficult for me to defend my less than excellent grades. A note from my Geometry teacher set off a parental emergency alert and Mom sat me down in the living room for a "heart to heart."

"Why are you doing so poorly in geometry?"

"Gee Mom, because of Helen, all the teachers expect me to do so much better. They don't even believe I'm Helen's brother."

"What does that have to do with your grade in geometry?"

"I'm in the back of the classroom and the teacher doesn't pay any attention to me."

"Look here bubelah, you may not use that as an excuse."

"Honestly Mom?"

"Yes, truth is good."

"By the time I get home after football practice and my work in the laundry, I'm too tired to finish my homework."

"If you want to continue playing football, you'd better buckle down on homework and study."

"I want to play football."

"Then, concentrate on your studies, because you must go to college. You know that don't you?"

"Yeah, I know. I'll really try – I promise."

To everyone's surprise; parents and teachers, including me, I opened books, studied hard, finished my homework, paid attention in class, and made the Honor Roll.

Prior to my senior year and my last high school football season, the big things expected of West Philly's football team were dashed, when our star tailback transferred to a prep school, the next best running back switched sports to soccer, and in the last week of the summer vacation, three of our biggest and best linemen were killed in an automobile accident returning from Atlantic City on New Jersey's White Horse Pike

Earlier in the year, in spring practice, I had made my mark and was almost certain to be a starter at linebacker and running back. Before the football season and our first preseason practice, my brothers and a crowd of fans and players watched as the coaches began to set up the starting single-wing offense.

"Eaton, line up at tailback," Wesley, the head coach directed. I moved into the tailback position.

"Wait a minute coach, you know, Geordie's not much of a passer," the assistant coach, Doug suggested.

"You're right. Okay, Eaton line up at fullback."

Billy groaned softly from the front of the crowd as I moved down to the fullback position.

"Don't you think we should have someone bigger at fullback?" Doug whispered.

"Hmm . . . okay . . . okay . . . Eaton, take the blocking back's position."

Billy's groan got louder as I moved further down to the blocking back's position.

Billy's groans drew all eyes to the littlest one in the crowd.

Wesley had had tried to ignore my little brother's groans, but this time he had to look around to see the groans' source. When the coach's eyes focused on Billy, he smiled.

"Is he your brother, kid?"

A defiant Billy said, "Yeah . . . and he's the best player you got!"

170

The entire crowd of coaches, players and onlookers burst into uproarious laughter. Billy's face turned red as a beet, and I wanted to climb into a hole.

Our first preseason scrimmage was against Penn Charter. In my first chance to run the ball from the single-wing quarterback's position, I was called to carry the ball into the center of the line.

During the entire scrimmage, the Penn Charter coach had been uncanny in his ability to diagnose our plays before we ran them.

Just as we lined up for my play, the Penn Charter's coach shouted, "Watch center!"

How did he know that? The ball was centered to me, but there was no place to run in the center of the line, and I was hit from all sides that caused me to fumble the ball. Penn Charter recovered my fumble and I returned to the huddle to face an angry coach.

"For Christ's sake Eaton, hold onto the damn ball!"

That became my last opportunity to run the ball for the rest of the scrimmage. As usual, my father was at the scrimmage, a fact that I would regret later that day at dinner.

Just as we sat down for dinner, Pop jibed me by mimicking the coach, "For Christ's sake Eaton, hold onto the damn ball!"

Feeling bad enough about my poor performance in the Penn Charter scrimmage, without thinking, I lashed back at my father,

"Please don't come to my practices – no other parents do. It's embarrassing."

That rebuke stung Pop more than I knew. In his hard working youth, my father never had the opportunity to play sports, and in a way he lived the game vicariously through me. In watching me play was something my father had thoroughly enjoyed.

A glum father responded to my declaration and said, "Okay with me, if that's the way you feel."

Unknowingly, I had deeply hurt my father's feelings. He had supported me in the face of Mom's opposition, attended practically every single high school and sandlot game and practice, tended to my game injuries, and this was how I showed my appreciation. At that instant, I didn't realize until later that my father had promised himself to never attend another one of my football practices or games.

West Philadelphia High's football season was a disappointment. I played well in the weak-side linebacker position, but because of that one fumble, the coach refused to call my number on offense. Over the years, Coach Wesley had developed the reputation as an innovator in football strategy, but the years had taken their toll on his enthusiasm for the game. The loss of key players before the season had further drained the coach's spirit, which had its effect on the entire team's morale as well.

In a game at Benjamin Franklin High, a predominantly colored school, I was surprised to see my teammates' lack of spirit. They were intimidated by the Ben Franklin team and its fans. The Benjamin Franklin players were a mean, threatening bunch and their fans sounded a lot like the crowd in Rome's Coliseum that roared their approval of the spectacle of Christians being devoured by lions. The crudeness and violence of sandlot football had inoculated me from trash talk and intimidation. I tuned out threats and insults and concentrated on playing my aggressive game.

I had my best game of the season; intercepting a pass, sacking the quarterback, and making solid tackles all over the field, but Ben Franklin beat us badly. On the bus ride from the game, my teammates showed no remorse from the beating we had just taken. They were laughing, grab-assing and singing.

Assistant Coach Douug seethed in anger from the lousy team play and how easily the loss was accepted. He stood up at the front of the bus and shouted, "STOP YOUR DAMN SINGING AND LAUGHING! You just got your asses kicked! You lost the damn game! Except for Eaton, you all played like a bunch of pussies."

The Ben Franklin game unveiled the team's lack of heart, as well as its failings in coaching. During the season, our team went through several formations. If we won a game with single wing

172

formations and a successful set of plays, the exact same formations and plays were used the following week. Our Head Coach was too lazy to come up with a new game plan and ignored the fact that we had been scouted by our next opponent. Our next opponent was fully prepared for every formation and play they had scouted. In the next game, the plays that were so successful in our last game failed miserably. Predictably, the West Philadelphia Speedboys took another beating.

After a loss, our coach switched to entirely different formations and a new set of plays for the following week's game. This poor strategy resulted in a .500 season, a far cry from the success that had been predicted for our team.

The last football game of the season and my high school career was on an unusually warm Thanksgiving Day against our archrival West Catholic High. Years ago, before the emergence of professional football, this traditional holiday game had attracted as many as 25,000 football fans at Shibe Park. Now, it was just another high school football game played in front of about a thousand or so fans, but still an important West Philadelphia area rivalry.

As fate would have it, the quarterback for West Catholic was my old nemesis from my sandlot football days, McClaren. McClaren hadn't noticed me, but I recognized him and relished the opportunity to get another crack at my sandlot foe. Looking intently in the stands, I spied my brothers, but to my severe disappointment, Pop wasn't with them, not even for my very last high school game.

The West Philly Speedboys scored in their first series, but missed the extra point. After West Philly's score, neither team could muster much of an offense. McClaren was still unaware that I was on the opposite side of the line. The clock was about to end the first half, when Quarterback McClaren launched a pass to his left end that had button-hooked ten yards downfield. I leaped up and managed to tip the ball to the ground.

173

In stretching for the ball, I felt a slight muscle spasm in my right calf. Because of the warm day, dehydration had caused the muscle cramp. In those days, football players weren't permitted to drink water during the game, "It'll give you stomach cramps."
In those days, it's a miracle more football players didn't collapse or die from heat exhaustion.

Simple muscle cramps weren't treated very well, because our so-called trainer was a high school student with no medical experience. As soon as I limped out to play the second half and attempted to jog on the sidelines, the coaches could see I couldn't run and benched me. Forlorn on the bench, I watched West Philly kick off to West Catholic. The West Catholic runner took the ball around the twenty yard line and ran straight up the middle of the field, my defensive lane on kickoffs, and ran untouched for a touchdown. Fortunately, the point after was missed and the score remained tied.

For the remainder of the second half neither team could dent the scoreboard. But in the game's closing minutes West Catholic generated a drive with McClaren's running and passing. On first down, a couple of running plays placed the ball on the one-yard line, and McClaren huddled the West Catholic team.

At this critical point, the coach shouted, "Eaton can you play?"

"You bet!" I shouted back as I ran with a limp onto the field before the coach could see that my leg was still cramped and try to stop me.

With the stadium clock winding down, only 8 seconds left in the game, I tuned my ear into the huddle and discovered that my sworn enemy hadn't changed his loudmouth frustrations in the huddle.

McClaren said, "Dammit–I'll take the goddamn ball over center! Block those bastards outta there!"

When the West Catholic team broke their huddle and lined up in their T formation, I slid slowly over center from my weak-side linebacker position. The clock clicked down, 10 . . . 9 . . . .

McClaren barked, "Down . . . Set . . . Hut one!"

The West Catholic center snapped the ball to McClaren, and the stadium clock clicked to 0. McClaren lowered his head to dive through a gaping hole that opened over center. Since I heard the play called, I bulled headlong into the opening before McClaren could take a step. McClaren had cradled the ball in his belly and I drove my helmet directly into the exposed ball. The pigskin bounced onto the turf.

"FUMBLE!"

Seeing the ball fly, I twisted my leg attempting to recover the fumble and felt a dagger-like pain in my cramped calf. The football bounced out of my reach, rolled crazily into the end zone, and was smothered by our safety. The ref's whistle signaled the game's end in a tie.

The West Philly players were relieved that the winning score was prevented and jumped up and down in the end zone. Our bench cleared and spilled onto the field, leading the charge of West Philly's fans out of the stands. I wasn't doing any jumping at the time, because my leg was too painful.

Still on the turf, a devastated McClaren was forced to listen to West Philly's celebration, and stayed down a few moments longer. Teary eyed, the West Catholic quarterback struggled to his feet and looked to see who had caused him to fumble. McClaren couldn't believe his eyes, when he saw that his old sandlot football nemesis was the tackler..

"NO! IT"S YOU! I never thought I'd see you again–you son-of-a-bitch!"

Without speaking, I smiled broadly and pointed to the scoreboard.

McClaren barked, "YOU, you bastard!"

Employing my best cat-ate-the-canary grin, I sneered "Yeah it's me, and a Happy Thanksgiving!"

Watching me turn and limp away, McClaren was red faced with rage and screamed to the heavens.

"JESUS! I can't believe it . . . it's that same Jew *bastard*!"

Ignoring my painful cramp, I limped off the field with an exhilarating feeling of satisfaction that I had finally settled my score with McClaren.

The Eatons' Thanksgiving dinner table groaned from the huge turkey and all the trimmings that Mom had prepared. In between mouthfuls of turkey, stuffing, and cranberry sauce, I was engrossed in thought about Pop's absence from the game. I finally asked the question that had been burning inside me for weeks.

"Pop, you haven't been to any of my high school games, but why weren't you at least at today's game against West Catholic? It was my last game and on your day-off too."

"You told me I embarrassed you, coming to watch you play . . . didn't you?"

"I only meant practices, but I'm sorry . . . I really am."

Pop's face lit up with a broad smile, he slid back from the table.

"Hot dog! HAH! I get an *apology from you – at last!*"

The realization of how much my words had hurt my father's feelings finally hit me. I got up and walked over to his chair and rested my hand on his shoulder.

"I'm really sorry. If I knew how badly you felt, I sure would've apologized a lot sooner."

Pop got up from his chair and clutched my shoulders.

"Come here sunshine."

Engulfed in my Pop's bear hug, we embraced for a long time. Tears welled up in Pop's eyes. He would have loved dearly to see his eldest son play, but a belated, big hug would have to do.

Ignoring the emotional moment, Billy leaned over to his mother.

"Mom, if I eat my green beans, can I have two helpings of pie?"

"Little one, eat your dinner first, and then we'll see about dessert. There's an old Yiddish expression, 'Khap nisht di lokshn far oh fish.' It means don't put the cart before the horse, but the literal translation is: Don't grab the noodles before the fish."

The rest of the dinner was full of happy, normal, family conversation, and this Thanksgiving Day dinner had a special meaning for me.

CHAPTER TWENTY-FIVE
THE ITALIAN GIRLS

While I was occupied with football, Bob had been busy searching for the best places to meet girls. He discovered a treasure trove at the Market Street's roller skating rink. He could hardly wait to tell Don, Si and me about the girls he met at the rink. On a Saturday afternoon and the football season was over, our guys were back at our usual place on the deli's steps.

"No joke - These girls I met at the roller skating rink are dolls!"

Don laughed, "HA! Big deal! You say that about all the girls you meet,"

I said, "I heard that rink skating is a hell of a lot different than street skates-I'll probably fall on my ass."

"Hey guys, don't be party poopers. I'm tellin' ya there's plenty of good lookin' girls and roller skating is fun. Sure, I fell down a few times, but finally got the hang of it. You can take your pick of Adele's friends, but Adele Ricci is mine. She's pretty with a terrific personality–a real doll."

My ears perked up, "Adele Ricci? She's Italian?

"Yeah, Adele and her friends are from South Philly. You'll like them–they're all lulus. I told Adele I'd bring some of my buddies tonight."

Roller skating was an interesting idea, but the thought of meeting Italian girls from South Philly was a totally different thing. Bob had left us astray before was a thought that made me hesitate. There was a lot to think about, but tackle football had altered my life, and this may be another new life-changing experience.

I summed up my thoughts and said, "Okay Bob, I think it might be fun, and it's gotta be better than doing nothin' on a Saturday night."

From the dark Market Street doorway, we stepped into the roller rink emporium and were immediately struck by a whole new world of bright lights and loud organ music. I'd never seen so many pretty girls in one place at one time. There was plenty of competition in guys too, but our eyes focused on the girls, lots of girls in cute short skirts.

Colored strobe lights played around the rink and pulsated to the beat of the organ music. There were all types of skaters in pairs and alone rolling around the rink. Besides the professional looking skaters that danced, spun and glided around effortlessly, there were the stumble bums, straight ahead skaters that dared not try anything fancy, but the majority appeared to have some of the basic dance and turn moves.

Bob looked at the three of us, "Welll . . .whatcha think?"

Si spouted, "Wow! This is great!"

"So far, so good," I said

"Where do all these beautiful girls come from?" Don enthused.

I couldn't help staring at the pretty girls that rolled by, but followed Bob's lead in getting rented rink skates and lacing them up. Standing up was a problem for Si and Don, but staying up was even more difficult for them. On his maiden voyage, Don's feet went in two directions and his arms flapped like a wounded Albatross as he floundered through a crowd of amused skaters, almost falling, but ending with a bump at the railing that bordered the rink.

I laughed and shouted to Don, "You looked awful!"

"Oh yeah, let's see [pant] what you can do smart guy?"

I was afraid I couldn't do much better than Don, but I learned a little from watching his maiden flight. I still stumbled and staggered, but miraculously joined Don at the rail without falling.

It was Don's turn to laugh.

"Hah! You looked pretty awful too."

179

Si didn't do much better on his maiden voyage, but he made it. Compared to us, Bob looked like a professional skater, gliding up and coming to a smooth stop.

"Now, whatcha think guys? Isn't this great? Have you ever seen so many cute girls?"

It was all new to me; bright colored lights, loud organ music, roller skates rumbling on the wooden rink, boys and girls streaming by together. Some were skillfully dancing, while others were barely staying upright. Most of the girls wore short-short skirts that revealed more leg than I had ever seen at West Philly high. Most high school girls wore skirts down to their ankles that covered their legs like a blanket, revealing only a mere glimpse of their bobby socks.

Bob's eyes lit up, "Here comes Adele!"

Skating toward us was a beautiful vision of a pretty dark haired girl with a terrific smile.

Adele glided up gracefully and came to a smooth stop at the rail.

"Hi, Bob!"

It was amazing to me that "Hi Bob" could sound so musical and effervescent.

She held out her slender hand to me and said, "Hi, I'm Adele."

I tried not to gush.

"Hi, I'm Geordie."

"It's great to see you again Bob, and I'm really happy that you brought your friends. I can't wait to introduce you all to my terrific girlfriends."

I liked Adele immediately, because I hadn't met anyone like her. Except for the redhead in my 5th grade class, I hadn't been this attracted to a girl. Not only did she possess a remarkably pretty, olive skin face, and a cute little turned-up nose, but I was struck by Adele's sparkling and bubbling personality.

"You've got to meet my girlfriends–wait here a minute." Adele informed us with a warm and infectious smile.

I looked longingly after Adele as she skated smoothly off to round up her friends.

"Me? I'm not going anyplace–in fact I don't dare move. You're right Bob . . . Adele's a dolla."

We laughed together and chorused, "Adele's a dolla, Adele's a dolla, Adele's a dolla!"

Noticing the dreamy look on my face, Bob thought he'd better remind me that Adele was his girl.

"Remember guys, Adele's mine. Don't worry, they're all dishes, you'll see,"

Bob didn't have to tell me that Adele was his girl-I was already cursing my luck. My mind went down the list of girls I had liked and my chances with them had fizzled.

A few minutes later, skating behind her, Adele and her three friends skated up to the railing. As Bob had promised, Adele's friends were pretty, petite, dark haired Italian girls, but they didn't have Adele's charisma. I'd never met anyone with her combination of unabashed friendliness, pretty appearance, and personality.

"Have you ever skated before?" Adele asked me.

"The minute you see me out there, you'll know I've never skated before."

Adele smiled and said, "Bob I'm going to show Geordie some of the roller skating basics."

Bob tried hard not to frown, curled his lips into a half smile and nodded.

"C'mon Geordie, I'll skate with you and keep you from falling."

Adele's encouragement was all that I needed, and I released my death grip from the railing. My maiden voyage onto the skating rink was plenty shaky at first, but I was determined not to fall and embarrass myself. Adele took both my hands in the pairing position, and we began to skate off together. She was very patient and gave me enough tips to keep me in a vertical position as we circled the floor in rhythm to the music. Before long, I became proficient and confident enough to skate with Adele's friends and skate solo, but I could never be classified as a good skater.

Mastering the smooth turns to skate backwards was an impossible feat for me. My bowed legs prevented me from being able to position my feet correctly: Heels back to back with feet in a straight line allowed a skater to swivel his/her feet and make a smooth turn to skate backwards. To make the turn to skate backwards, I had to hop from front to back, which led to more than a few embarrassing falls. The fact that I could skate in pairs with a girl and not fall on my face had to be good enough.

There was hardly a Saturday that Don, Si, Bob and I didn't meet with the Italian girls at the skating rink. Except for Bob's pairing off with Adele, the rest of us intermingled, which was fun, but not what I really wanted. Every chance I could get, I'd invite Adele to skate around the rink with me, but as long as she was "Bob's girl," I was far from satisfied.

After several weeks had passed, Adele said, "I'd like to have everyone come to my house for a party."

"I can get Dad's car and I can drive the guys into South Philly," Don said.

"That's terrific," Bob said in hugging Adele.

Si and I looked at each other, not certain about getting approval from our parents, but we stammered together, "Uh . . . sure . . . that'd be great."

Mom' reaction wasn't so great. When she learned that Si and I had been invited to a party with Italian girls in South Philadelphia, the matzoh hit the fan in the Eaton household. The Jewish mother was more concerned that her eldest son was "mixed up" with an Italian-Catholic girl. She didn't seem to think that my younger brother, Si's involvement with the Italian girls was a threat.

"Oy, vai iz mir – first he's playing football with Irish Catholics, now he's going with Italian Catholic shiksehs!" George, you must talk to Geordie! What's the matter with him? Why not a nice Jewish girl? Is he meshugeh?"

182

Pope said with a smile, "I'll talk to him, but I don't promise that I'll suggest a nice Jewish girl." Then he ducked to avoid his wife's playful slap.

In the living room, I was apprehensive that my father had asked to speak with me alone. While I sat on the sofa, I nervously tied and retied my sneakers' shoelaces until my father appeared and sank into his recliner.

"Look here Sunshine, I had to fight like hell to get away from South Philadelphia, and now you're going back there to party with Italian girls."

"But Dad, they're great girls and we're having a lot of fun together. Honest . . . there's nothing serious going on." I said this with sincerity, because there really wasn't anything serious going on.

My going to a party in South Philadelphia with Italian girls brought back bitter memories of years of struggle and hardship for Pop. He had led a hard life growing up in South Philadelphia, helping his mother scrape out a living in her bread making business and delivering her bread in a horse and wagon in all kinds of weather. But what hurt him most was the shame he felt in being forced to return with his family to live in South Philadelphia after his radio repair business failed in the depths of the Great Depression.

Until my father secured the radio technician job in West Philadelphia, the depression years in South Philadelphia were terribly lean years. In my father's mind, South Philadelphia, being predominantly Italian, made tough times synonymous with South Philadelphian Italians. My parents were determined that all their children would be college educated and go on to lead successful adult lives. Anything that might detract from that objective was considered a threat.

After much pleading and assurances, my father realized that his arguments weren't going to do much to sway me. In reality, he was happy that football had helped my confidence and concluded that going with Italian girls from South Philadelphia might not be so bad for me. He decided that his eldest son's interest in girls, even Italian girls, was just another phase in his maturity.

"Okay, Geordie. As long as you say it's not serious, I don't see that it's a problem. You know your mother, but I'll try to calm her down."

Into the kitchen trudged my father with full knowledge that he had a hard sell ahead of him. Pop recapped our discussion and began a longwinded explanation of the pros and cons of my socializing with Italian girls from South Philadelphia. He neglected to mention that he had ended up siding with me.

"I spoke to him about . . . ."

"Stop there! All I want to know is . . . did you or did you not tell him that we forbid him going to a party in South Philadelphia? You know, George, you remind me of an old Yiddish expression, *Hakn a tshaynik.*"

"I'm sure you're going to tell me what that means."

"It means to be longwinded, literally to bang on a tea kettle. Please, George, get to the point."

"I believe that we should let him have some fun. He says that they're nice girls and it's not serious. Fannie, I think we should let boys be boys."

"Oy!" Without another word, Mom sank down into a kitchen chair and rested her elbows onto the table, hands covering her face. The Rabbi's daughter felt the full weight of her hopes and principles slipping away, one by one. I imagine it was the same feeling that Tevya in the *Fiddler on the Roof* musical, when traditions were slipping away.

Realizing that there was little more he could do or say that would console his wife, her husband retreated to the living room and his recliner. He settled back in his recliner, picked up a radio magazine to read about the future of electronics. For my father, reading about the future of electronics was educational and interesting, but not quite stimulating enough to ward off fatigue from long work days. He succumbed and dozed off.

The party at Adele's house led to other dance parties at Adele's and her friends' homes. We slow danced with the girls to popular music, terrific ballads by great singers: Al Martino's *"Here in my Heart"*, Tony Bennet's *"Because of You"* and *Cold Cold Heart"*, Johnny Ray's *Little White Cloud"*, Patty Page's *"Tennessee Walt"* was just some of the great slow dance music in the 50s

I had become a pretty good at the two-step from dances on Saturday nights in up-state Pennsylvania, at the Wyoming Methodist Camp Ground. Don's parents owned a summer cottage in the hills above Wyoming, PA. After Saturday nights' square dances, ballads were played for dancing. That's where I learned to spin, dip, and all the stuff that looks good.

Any time I had the chance to dance with Adele to a song like Tony Bennett's, *Because of You*, the words *"there's a song in my heart"* had a special meaning for me. Over the year, we continued to roller skate, bowl and party with the pretty Italian girls from South Philadelphia, but Adele remained Bob's girl.

CHAPTER TWENTY-SIX
IVY LEAGUE FOOTBALL

Even though my sister and mother had graduated from the University of Pennsylvania, I was prepared to matriculate at Drexel Tech, if I was offered a football scholarship. In my interview with Drexel Tech's football coach, he made it painfully clear to me that a 155 pound, 5'9" linebacker wasn't the best scholarship prospect, not even for a small college like Drexel.
Rejection by Drexel's football coach drove me to enroll at Ivy League Penn.

Entry into college and my age created new challenges for the Eaton family. I was getting only average grades in the college of arts and sciences' spring courses, and my 18th birthday made me eligible to be drafted to fight in a raging Korean War. Only the top one-third of a college class was exempt from the draft, which made my parents fearful that I might not keep my grades up, and I'd become the Korean War's "draft bait."

Not able to accept the risk that her eldest son might be shipped to a foreign land to fight in a deadly and unpopular war, my mother took the proverbial bull by the horns and assumed command of my future. One morning, my mother escorted me up Locust Street to the new Wharton School of Business' building on Locust Street where I was enrolled in a business curriculum. She then she marched me over to the NROTC building on Walnut Street to enlist me in Penn's NROTC program.

Within a single morning, the matriarch had set my future on a positive course. There would be no more floundering around without a purpose in the college of arts and sciences. Enrollment in Wharton offered me the opportunity for a business career, and enlistment in the NROTC assured me of an uninterrupted college education with an important exemption from the draft.

186

The Fall Semester had just begun and I was engrossed in reading the *Daily Pennsylvanian* while sitting in Penn's student center, Houston Hall. I hesitated in my reading, when I came upon an article that quoted the freshman football coach's desire for more players. Up to that point, I hadn't considered playing football, certainly not at Penn. If Drexel wasn't interested in me, I didn't think I'd have a chance to play in a major football program like Penn's.

The Daily Pennsylvania's article was the catalyst that made me decide to give college football a shot. There would be a problem, because I had worked the entire summer at my cousin, Lou Bender's plastics plant downtown. It was a source for spending money and college tuition, and I'd have to choose between my job and football. After a brief deliberation, the desire to return to football outweighed all other considerations–I opted for football.

At the dinner table, on hearing my decision to join Penn's freshman team, Mom expressed her concerns, "What are you saying? What about your job with Lou? I can't believe it! Son, have mercy on me!" What about your schoolwork? George, talk to your son!"

"If that's what he wants to do, and as long as he keeps up with his studies, I don't see any harm in his playing football at Penn. He's not playing football with the Ludlow Street crowd is he?"

My exasperated mother sighed, "Again . . . I should have known that you'd be of little help to me."

"Do you really think you're gonna be able to play for Penn's team," Si asked.

"Sure he can – he's good!" Billy shouted.

"Thanks little brother. Mom, I want to give it a try. If I don't make the team, I'll go back to work. I promise I'll hit the books too."

Mom saw she was fighting a losing battle, "What will you do for money?"

"Don't worry – I saved a little from my summer job."

Mom sighed, "This reminds me of an old Yiddish saying."

The family leaned forward over the dinner table. We thoroughly enjoyed the old Yiddish sayings.

"Got helft dem oremair: Er farhit im fun tazere aveyres. God helps the poor man: He protects him from expensive sins."

My mother's Yiddish saying wasn't exactly inspiring, but it would have to do, because whatever the meaning I was determined to go out for Penn's football team.

The gray stone athletic building stood in the shadow of Penn's Franklin Field, a red brick structure and home for the University of Pennsylvania Quakers' football games, the annual Army-Navy football games and the Penn Relays. The stadium was built in 1922 and sat 78,000 red and blue football fans. The ivy covered athletic building and its old, dingy offices looked as if Benjamin Franklin, Penn's founder, still paced the halls.

Making my way down a dimly lit hallway, I reached the equally dim Freshman Coach's office. The only light was a sunray beam that fell upon a desk surface covered with mounds of papers and binders. Various pieces of Football gear were scattered around, adding to the overall impression of disarray. The office furnishings were as fatigued looking as the freshman team's coach, whose feet were propped on the desk, and his tall, lean body was stretched so far back in a chair it appeared he could easily fall backwards. It appeared to me that the coach was taking a nap or close to one.

"Excuse me coach."

The coach stirred upright in his chair. "Huh . . . whatcha want son?"

"The Daily Pennsylvania said that the Freshman Team needed players and I'd like to play."

The coach sleepily eyed me up and down.

"Oh . . . yeah, what makes you think you can play for Penn? [Yawn] Any experience?"

"I was a back on offense and started at linebacker at West Philly High."

"Linebacker you say [yawn]? You were a starter [yawn]? What's your name [yawn]?"

"George Eaton. Yes sir, but I think I'd like to try out at a defensive back position, because I may be too small for a college linebacker."

"[Yawn], okay son. Pickup your equipment down the hall and practice starts at four."

"Thanks a lot!"

I couldn't believe that I had been given a chance to play for Penn. I spun around and bounced out of the office, hardly able to contain my excitement. The freshman coach looked sleepily at the happy, departing recruit and shook his head. My size was unimpressive, especially for a linebacker, but he thought that the new recruit might be useful as cannon fodder in practices. He slumped back in his chair to resume his nap.

On my first day on the practice field, I saw at once the hurdles I faced. First off, scholarship players didn't hide their disdain for walk-ons. Secondly, the freshmen players were big and tough men heavily recruited from the hard coal regions of up-state Pennsylvania. Football was a blood sport in those areas of the state, and many of Penn's recruits were products of coal mining families with names that ended in "ski."

Sports magazine had just published an article titled, *Is Penn Too Big for the Ivy League?* The Pennsylvania Quakers dominated Ivy League opponents and had stayed competitive with major football programs by recruiting All American quality football players like Bernie Lemonick, Chuck Bedenarik, and Eddie Bell. Bob Evans was a huge tackle and a senior on this year's Varsity Team, and he appeared to be a shoo-in for All American honors.

Thankfully, another walk-on took some of the heat off me and bore the brunt of the scholarship players' scorn. He was the grandson of Bayer, one of Penn's all-time football greats. The problem was he wasn't fortunate enough to inherit his grandfather's athletic genes. He was a short, skinny, spectacled drop-kicker, but certainly not a football player. Drop-kicking had disappeared from football for many years, but that was all that the grandson could do to participate in the game of football. It was obvious that the drop-kicker really didn't want to be there, but the grandfather's endowment to Penn insured the grandson's place on the freshman team.

But I had my own problems with the scholarship players. In scrimmages, when my number was called to run the ball, the quarterback's handoff was invariably late, and passes were overthrown or thrown behind me. On defense I repeatedly broke up plays with good hard tackling that frustrated the highly touted freshmen running backs. Instead of praising me, the coaches were annoyed that I messed up their plays and called for me to be double-teamed. I opened the coaches' eyes on one particular play, when I was blocked to my knees by two of the biggest linemen. Still on my knees, I reached out and grabbed enough of the passing ball carrier's legs to trip him up.

After weeks of practice, I was able to garner a modicum of respect from the scholarship freshmen and the coaches, and traveled overnight by train to Ithaca, NY for our game with Cornell. Shivering in the snow along the Cayuga River, I shivered watching and watching the game. I spent a lot of time watching and shivering, and I waited for my name to be called to go in the game, but the call never came.

A week later, I got my first opportunity to play against Columbia at home on our practice field. Entering the game at linebacker, I felt right at home in the position, and I was in on several tackles. Unfortunately, the coach recalled that I wanted to convert myself to a defensive back, and he moved me to cornerback where I was like a fish out of water. On two successive plays, Columbia's quarterback ran end sweeps. I wrongly believed they were running plays and ran up to stop the run, but the Quarterback pulled up to throw passes over my head to receivers for touchdowns. I was benched for the rest of the game.

In the closing minutes of the Columbia game, we had increased our lead to 34-14. Our coach saw this as an opportunity to placate the esteemed alumnus, who had been breathing down his neck.

He pointed to the drop-kicker, "You! Get in there and kick the extra point!"

"Me?"

"Yeah, you!"

The sight of the skinny, little, spectacled player entering the game infuriated the Columbia team. The Columbia Lions thought that Penn was trying to rub it in by sending in this joke of a player. In their defensive huddle, the Lions were roaring.

"Look, the little son-of-a-bitch ain't even wearing shoulder pads. Those damn Penn guys are laughing at us! Kill that little bastard!"

On seeing Bayer III coming in from the sideline to kick the extra point, Penn's huddle reached an instant consensus.

"Nobody blocks for that pansy – you hear me!"

This was to be a great practical joke and the huddle broke into hysterics. When the drop-kicker arrived in the huddle, he was nervous as hell and wondered what all the laughing was about. Meanwhile, the Columbia players became certain that they were the butt of a Penn joke, and the laughter in Penn's huddle confirmed their suspicions.

"KILL 'IM!" The Columbia Lions roared.

The two teams lined up for the extra point kick. Penn's walk-on and nervous drop-kicker stood ten yards behind the center all by himself, shaking in readiness to take the snap from center. The Columbia linemen growled and pawed the ground.

"LET'S STICK IT IN HIS EAR!"

Hearing threats to do him serious, bodily harm made the kicker even shakier. It didn't go unnoticed by the Lions that the Penn players seemed to be relishing and smiling over some secret joke.

On the ball's snap, the Lions came with an eleven-man rush. They charged like wild, angry beasts to devour our kicker. To

Columbia's surprise, Penn's linemen and blocking backs performed like matadors, and no one attempted to block or even slow their angry rush. The little, skinny drop-kicker didn't have a chance, and the instant the center snap reached the defenseless kicker, he was engulfed by the entire Columbia team. The collision between eleven large men and a sprig of a human being resembled a catastrophic train wreck.

When they peeled away the Lions players, the shattered remains of the all-time great's grandson lay lifeless on the turf. The coaches and trainers ran onto the field to tend to the prostrate drop kicker. After ten minutes or so and several whiffs of smelling salts, Penn's last known drop-kicker regained consciousness and was helped to his feet. His legs weren't operational. With the assistance of two trainers, the wounded warrior was dragged off the field, never to be seen again by Penn's freshman football team.

The team that conspired against the drop-kicking walk-on felt no hint of remorse for their scheme that almost killed him. They gloated over the "pussy's" departure from the team. For several weeks after the Columbia game, I overheard the scholarship players whispering, recalling what a great joke they had played on the little drop-kicker and burst into raucous laughter. For certain, I didn't join in their merriment, because I felt that these guys would just as soon laugh at my funeral and only "By the grace of God, there go I."

The Frosh team was the guinea pig for the varsity in scrimmages in preparation for the varsity's next game. We'd run the next week's opponent's offensive plays and set up in their defensive formations. Back in my familiar position at the weak-side linebacker position, I had the instincts to avoid blocks and plug holes before the runners could break through the line. On offense, I was rarely called on to run the ball, but blocked well enough. However, on one offensive pass play, my half-back assignment was to protect the passer on any rush from the right side. All American tackle, Bob Evans, who outweighed me by at least 100 pounds, came crashing in from the right. I threw my shoulders at the rushing tackle's legs.

BOING!

It was as if I collided with an Oak tree. I bounced off the All American tackle's trunk-like legs, and Bob Evans ran through me as if I wasn't there.

In that football era, weight training didn't exist from sandlot to professional football. The weight training theory was: "You don't want to lift weights it'll make you too muscle bound to play football." Without weight strengthening, a freshman of my size and maturity couldn't possibly counter an older player of superior size and weight like an All American Bob Evans. In today's football, through weight training, players of my age, height, and frame can weigh 50 pounds more with much greater strength.

Still, I had gained stature in the coaches' eyes. "That Eaton kid may be small, but he can sure tackle." Even the first-string, scholarship players came to recognize me for gutsy play. As a result, I was ecstatic when I learned that I was named to be the second-string linebacker in our game versus Princeton, and the game would be played in Franklin Field.

Years back, on the deli's steps, I had mused that one day maybe I could play on Franklin Field and here would be my first opportunity. But my joy was short-lived, because I learned that the Saturday I was to play in the Princeton game conflicted with the time I would be on an NROTC cruise to Bermuda. I had signed up for the cruise months before without knowledge of the Frosh football team's schedule. Several other freshman players had made the same mistake. The NROTC Commandant decided to administer military discipline, and refused to release me and the others from the cruise. When I signed up for the cruise to Bermuda, it sounded like a great opportunity, but it became a huge disappointment. I would lose my opportunity to play in

Franklin Field, but the lost football opportunity would be the least of my problems.

CHAPTER TWENTY- SEVEN
THE BERMUDA TRANGLE

The four of us were at the bowling alley on Chestnut Street and in good humor. We watched Bob crouch with a bowling ball in hand and prepare to make his approach to the line.

"Don't choke Bob!" I shouted from the bench.

"Shut up, Geordie! I'm concentrating."

Bob took three steps in his approach and released the ball straight down the middle of the alley. The ball hit the head pin and the pins went flying, leaving the deadly 7-10 split.

"See what your talking did to me," Bob growled and glared back at me sitting with Don and Adele on the bowling alley's bench.

"Hey, don't blame the split on me."

From the ball return, Bob gave me another dirty look.

Adele gushed, "Wow, Geordie you're so lucky! A cruise to Bermuda - you're going to come back with a beautiful tan."

"Honestly, I'd rather be playing football in Franklin Field. To make matters worse, freshman games are normally played down on the practice field–this was gonna be something special."

Adele put her arm around my shoulder and kissed me on the cheek.

"Look at the bright side: A nice cruise, basking in Bermuda's sun, and seeing some great sights. People say Bermuda's beautiful and you'll have a great time."

Even the warmth of Adele's kiss couldn't shake me from my doldrums.

Bristling at seeing Adele's kiss, Bob promptly threw a gutter ball.

Don laughed, "That was terrible!"

Everyone laughed as Bob stomped back. He wasn't sure whether he was angrier at Adele kissing me or throwing a gutter ball. Bob flopped on the bench beside me and he blurted, "Just don't get seasick."

"I've only been seasick a couple of times, and only when I went deep sea fishing with my Pop in a small fishing boat. When we trolled for flounder, I really got sick and heaved my guts out. I'd catch a fish, feed the fish, then catch a fish, feed the fish."

Don said, "Don't worry, you'll be on a big ship-you probably won't get seasick at all."

"I guess so. Anyway, I have no choice, because the Navy says I've got to go."

I was in a deep funk. I didn't bowl well and wasn't much fun for the rest of the evening. All I could do was curse my misfortune. I had finally impressed the coaches enough to be put in the Franklin Field lineup, and now I wasn't able to play the game.

A week later, standing on the dock at the Philadelphia Naval Shipyard, I was disheartened when I caught sight of my cruise ship to Bermuda. My spirits were already beyond despair, but plummeted further. The ship that I was about to board was the PCE510, a Patrol Craft Escort, the smallest fighting ship in the Navy's arsenal. It didn't even have a name, just a number. That wasn't the worst of it. I and about one hundred NROTC midshipmen filed onto the so-called "ship" to discover that we would be crammed into a woefully undersized sleeping compartment, and we were to be stacked like pancakes in three-high bunks.

I moaned, "You've gotta be kidding."

Grumbling could be heard throughout the bunks' compartment, which assured me that I wasn't the only one that was disappointed in our cruise accommodations.

Just before dusk, the mooring lines were released and the Bermuda cruise was underway. I learned that I was assigned to four on–eight off watches in the engine room. At dinner, the Mess Hall's food was passable, and I felt that the engine room watch could be interesting. In an attempt to make the most of a bad situation, I told myself that maybe the whole cruise thing wasn't going to be so awful. As the evening fell, the PCE510, loaded with NROTC midshipmen, slowly plowed down the Delaware River into the Delaware Bay, headed out to the open sea, and into the Atlantic Ocean.

My first watch was the eight to midnight along with two other midshipmen and the engineer, Petty Officer Third Class Conroy. The engine room was deafening, reeked of diesel fuel and was stifling hot, but the hourly checks and logging of gauges kept the duty from being too boring. After initial instructions, the grizzled, rail-thin engineer never spoke another word to me or his other midshipmen assistants. At the beginning of the watch, the engineer took his position on a high stool and never moved from his perch for the entire watch's four hour period.

The sailor slumped on the stool and his eyes appeared to be completely closed, a picture of complete relaxation. It wasn't long before we discovered that he wasn't asleep. If one of us overlooked a gauge and failed to log a reading, the engineer opened one eye, grunted loudly, and emphatically pointed a finger in the direction of the missed meter. Relieved from my first watch at midnight, I returned to my bunk exhausted. The cramped, middle bunk didn't prevent me from falling asleep the instant my head hit the thin, hard mattress.

"GET UP EATON! You've got the next watch!"

Some insensitive bastard was shaking me and yelling in my ear, waking me from a beautiful dream about Adele.

"Okay, okay, you don't have to shout. I'm getting up! I grumbled.

Once I regained my senses, I realized that the ship was rocking and I was being tossed from side to side in my bunk. Out of the bunk and landing with both feet on the cold, steel deck, I felt the ship shuddering from side to side and going up and down like an out of control, carnival ride. Because I hadn't bothered to undress, I needed only to put on my shoes and socks. The ship's extreme movements made even that simple task difficult. On the way to the ship's Head (lavatory), the undulating deck beneath my feet forced me to stagger like a drunken sailor.

I questioned a Midshipman, who lurched along beside me.

"Damn! What the hell's going on?"

"I heard from a sailor that we're in the middle of a big storm off Cape Hatteras."

"There's a storm? That's just *great*-what *else* can go wrong?"

Before the Head's entrance, I was surprised to stumble into a long line of sailors and midshipmen. Why did everyone have to take a piss at the same time? Finally, when it was my turn at a urinal, I discovered that it wasn't the sound of pissing I heard–it was retching. It wasn't just urine that repulsed my senses–the stench was urine and vomit. I found myself in the midst of a mass of seasick humanity. I tried my best to piss in the direction of the urinal, but the ship's movements made me miss my target more often than not. Even brushing teeth was difficult, but shaving was impossible . . . unless I didn't mind losing an ear.

The ship continued to rock violently, making the climb down the ladders to the engine room treacherous. At times, only my deathlike grip on the railings saved me from hurtling to the deck below. Our Petty Officer Conroy had already taken up his position on the stool and looked as relaxed as ever, even though his stool teetered precariously with every roll of the ship. Masterfully, seemingly effortlessly, he shifted his body's weight and remained seated and relaxed on the tilting stool. Happy to reach the engine room in one piece, I took a quick glance at my two midshipmen watch-mates. They were ashen and had sprawled out on the engine room's deck. Boy, am I glad I'm not as sick as those two, I thought. At first, I sat in a chair, but soon realized that the ship's movement made sitting in a chair too difficult.

"Damn! Sitting in a chair is impossible isn't it? How in the hell does he manage to stay on that stool and look so relaxed doing it? I guess I better sit on the deck along with you guys."

They were too sick to utter a word in response, and I joined my fellow midshipmen on the engine room's steel deck.

"You know guys, I think I'm beginning to feel a little sick too."

My fellow midshipmen were too sick to acknowledge me and didn't try. Their faces had turned from gray to green and one after the other heaved their guts out in a nearby bucket.

"Now, I'm really getting nauseous."

The combination of the ship's movement, the engineer's swaying on his stool, the stifling heat of the engine room, the odor of diesel fuel, and the sight and smell of my vomiting shipmates finally made me succumb to the deadly seasickness.

"I better lie down."

I was in the throes of full-fledged seasickness and sought relief by laying flat on the cold, steel deck. I was too far gone and vomited uncontrollably in the designated vomit bucket. From that point on, for the remainder of the watch, I took turns with the other midshipmen to stagger around the engine room on the hour to post various gauge readings in the engine room's log, only to lie back down on the deck, and heave into the vomit bucket.

Day after day went by, but the thought of eating never crossed my mind. I went from lying in the engine room to lying in my bunk, and back to lying in the engine room. Accompanied by my midshipmen companions, we remained prone on the grated steel deck where we dry heaved in a bucket, and only got up to stagger through the log readings. On the first full day of this ordeal, I was afraid I was going to die. By the second day, I longed for a quick death.

On the third day of the little ship's rocking and rolling through the raging seas, I was still sick as a dog and still lying face down on the engine room's deck, when I heard, "Are you sick son?"

Was I dead? Was that God talking to me? No, it was the voice of a ship's officer, one of the few on the ship that wasn't sick. He bent over me and lifted my head off the deck.

I croaked a faint response, "Yes sir! You bet . . . I . . . am!"

With that, the officer grabbed me by the scruff of my neck and pulled me to my feet. Unfazed, Conroy didn't blink an eye and never stirred from his stool, as he watched his three assistants being hauled out of the engine room by the officer and a couple of seamen. I was practically dragged to the ship's Sick Bay.

When we reached the Sick Bay, the rescuing officer said, "Stay in line midshipmen. The corpsman will give you some pills." He then left to rescue some other poor souls.

The line of sick midshipmen and crew moved quickly, and it became my turn to face the corpsman. The corpsman's pallor didn't look much better than mine.

"Hold out your hand [Burp]!"

The corpsman reached into a jar of pills and thrust a number of pills into my outstretched hand and said, "Take two now [Burp]!"

He hesitated for a moment, turned an ugly shade of green, and bent down to throw up into a bucket at his feet.

"AAACK!"

Hardly missing a beat, the corpsman took his head out of the bucket and resumed his instructions, "Take one every four hours."

Not long after taking the two pills an absolute miracle occurred-I came back to life. Life was good again. The nausea had vanished, and I instantly became ravenous. Even the seas cooperated, because the ship had finally passed through the edge of the storm. A warm, bright sun broke through the clouds. My first stop was the mess hall where I grabbed the first piece of food I could see. My treasure was a grapefruit from a pile of fruit on a mess hall table. Taking my prize up the ladder, out into the fresh air and warm sun, onto the ship's fantail, I peeled and devoured the grapefruit in a flash–nothing had *ever* tasted quite so good to me. The salt air, sun and food restored my will to live–it was exhilarating.

Sunny, warm Bermuda was not to be. Both days spent in Bermuda were scarred by a steady, dismal rain. No football at

Franklin Field, deadly seasickness, a rain soaked Bermuda–it couldn't get worse. Not so, the Navy could make it even worse. The NROTC midshipmen were on this cruise to learn what the Navy was all about. Therefore, on the return to the Philadelphia Naval Shipyard, my fellow midshipmen and I were kept busy chipping and painting the ship from stem to stern. Since I had been assigned to the engine room, I helped paint the entire engine room. At least the midshipmen that painted the main deck got some sun.

All the way back to Philadelphia, in the boiling hot, smelly engine room, I bitched and painted, painted and bitched. During the entire cruise, except for the time I had eaten that one grapefruit on the ship's fantail, I hadn't had a glimpse of the sun.

When the PCE510 returned to dock at the Philadelphia Naval Shipyard, a host of thin disgruntled midshipmen shuffled down the gangway. At the moment, I was so angry about the disastrous cruise to Bermuda, I didn't consider the alternative. I could have suffered frostbite or worse in the war against the Chinese and North Korean communists.

A few days after returning from my doomed cruise to Bermuda, Don drove Bob, Si, and me in his family's car to South Philadelphia to see Adele. On the drive, I gave the guys all the gory details of the cruise from hell.

"God, Geordie, that was awful," Don said in sympathy.

"Adele told us that we had to bring you to see her as soon as you got home," Bob said and laughed loudly, "She thinks that you had a great time."

Don began to laugh so hard that he had to swerve from hitting an oncoming car.

I didn't appreciate their humor and gritted my teeth.

"Shaddup guys – you're not funny! Don, for Christ's sake, can't you watch where you're driving?!"

Adele answered the doorbell and greeted our group with her usual fabulous smile and effusive personality.

"Geordie, you're back! With a tan, you look grea-a-a . . . "

Entering the house, Adele got a better look at me in the light and saw that I had no tan, my face was as pale as a ghost, and my cheeks were sunken in from losing ten pounds.

"My God Geordie, what happened to you?!"

I proceeded to describe the horrible details of my first naval cruise to a very sympathetic listener in Adele. She rested her hand on my knee and listened to every word of my sad story. When I finished my tale of woe, Adele hugged me like never before and I hugged back. Even though Bob and Adele's relationship hadn't advanced beyond a strong friendship, Adele's attention to me made Bob envious. Now, he wished he had joined me on that lousy cruise.

The rest of the Freshman Football team's season was lost to me. There was only one other game on our schedule, but missing the Princeton game at Franklin Field caused the coaches to ignore me for the rest of the season. The hardest thing for me to do was to return to my cousin's plastic manufacturing plant and ask for my job back. Fortunately for me, my cousin merely scolded me for choosing football over the job, but allowed me to return.

After football, my weekly routine consisted of a full day of classes at Penn and some intra mural basketball, and I then took a trolley ride downtown to work at the plastics plant where I molded and trimmed plastic refrigerator panels, beer signs, and Esterbrook pen sets. On weekends and the following summer, I worked full-time at the plant.

On one critical summer day, I was operating a press that made bases for Esterbrook pen sets and worrying about the need to tell my cousin that I hoped to take time off to play Penn football in a couple of weeks. I came out of my thoughts, when I noticed the piece of hot plastic I had just laid over the plaster base had a hole on its edge. I had already started the press on its downward path, and I tried to adjust the plastic. It was too late, and I decided to stop the press, but the lever spun free and the press crushed my right index finger into the hot plastic.

"OWWW!!! HELP!"

The crushed and burning finger was extremely painful. At the sound of my pained cries, the foreman, Tony came running. He quickly discovered that the lever's nut had loosened and a wrench was needed.

"Hold on Geordie, I gotta get a wrench."

Tony ran off to retrieve a wrench and seconds later returned to tighten the nut and raised the press to release my crushed and burnt finger.

Tony walked with me six blocks to the hospital's emergency room. He had never forgiven me for leaving the plant in the lurch, when I left to play football in my freshman year. While we walked, Tony realized that my finger must be horribly painful and I hadn't let out a whimper.

"Geordie, I gotta admit you're one tough guy. I'm sorry I was hard on you for leaving us to play football. Now, I see that you've got the guts to play the game."

"Thanks Tony. You're right, I like football a lot, but this will probably kill my chances to play this year."

The recovery from the crushed burned finger ended thoughts of playing football in my sophomore year at Penn. It took six weeks before the bandages could be removed and the finger healed, but Penn' football was well into its season and out of my grasp.

I resigned myself to limit my sports to playing intra mural basketball for the NROTC team. With the lost opportunity of playing varsity football, each morning I staggered out of bed to walk to an 8:00 AM class at Penn. After classes, I took the trolley downtown to work at the plastic plant. My life had become monotonous, and I began to question my future at Penn. Why continue to go to Penn, if I can't play football? This question came up at the dinner table and my parents reacted angrily.

Pop demanded, "What do you mean, quitting college?"

Mom burst into tears, "Got zol ophitn! God forbid! You must go to college–it's your future. You don't want to be shipped to Korea-do you?"

I hadn't given much thought that Korea was the alternative to college and the NROTC, but even the thought of Korea may not be so bad compared to my dull life at work and in college. Football was my real love and I felt cheated. In any case, I realized that I'd better not bring up the subject again to my parents. If I was going to drop out, I'll just have to do it and then bear my parents' grief.

Because of work at my cousin's plant and Bob and Don were occupied with their own issues, we hadn't stayed in touch with Adele and her friends. That's why I was overwhelmed to bump into Adele in Houston Hall.

"Adele, wow it's great to see you! Are you going to Penn now?"

"Yes, you would know that, if you would have called me. By choosing Penn, I thought maybe we could see each other more often, if ever!" "Why haven't you called me?"

"Why haven't you called me?"

This was news to me. Is it possible that Della had the same feelings for me as I had for her?

"That'd be something, if you came to Penn on account of me, and I'm thinking of dropping out."

"Why in the world would you do that?"

"I didn't say for certain–I'm thinking about it."

"You've got to tell me that you won't."

Now was the time for me to tell to tell Adele how I felt about her.

"Adele, I . . ."

"Sorry, Geordie, as much as I'd love to talk, but I have a busy schedule today with classes and Penn's theater group. I'd really be disappointed, if you quit school. I wish I had time to chat, but I've got to run to a class. Call me!""

As I watched Adele disappear into the stream of students coming and going in Houston Hall, all I could think that there goes another missed opportunity,

CHAPTER TWENTY-EIGHT
SEMI-PRO FOOTBALL

Who was ringing the doorbell this early on a Saturday morning? When I got to the door, I was surprised to see Harry's smiling face.

"What's going on Harry?"

"Punch . . . uh, uh, Geordie, we need you to play for the 49ers today. We got a big game with some team in North Philly."

"Today you say and a team in North Philly? "Harry, you know I haven't played football for more than a year and I haven't played with you guys for three years–why now?"

"It ain't that we didn't want you to play with us. We were afraid you wouldn't play, but since you're not playing for Penn and your finger's healed, we thought you might like to play. Don told me that you may even quit Penn, so maybe you could play for us in some games. This is our first game this year, and it's a *big game!* We're gonna play in a real football stadium, referees and everything!"

For several minutes, I was seriously conflicted, pondering the idea of ever again playing football and certainly not with the 49ers.

"Gee, this is crazy. I don't know."

"Ah, c'mon Geordie, it'll be fun and we really need you."

"I don't think I've got any equipment at all."

"No problem. We've got everything you need."

The idea of playing with Eagles again had never entered my mind. Did I want to play football badly enough that I would return to play with them? I guess so.

"Okay, let me get my cleats and I'll go with you."

"Terrific! I'll wait on the porch."

Reentering the house, I thought it wouldn't be smart to tell Mom that I was going to play football, but I told her anyway.

"Mom, the 49ers need me to play today."

"WHAT!" "You can't be serious. Vai iz mir! It hasn't been a month, since your bandages were removed. Are you meshugeh?"

"My finger's fine. I haven't played football for a long time, and I'd really like to play today. It should be fun."

"Vos iz mit dir? Hob rakhnones!"

Mom was distraught and again resorted to Yiddish. For emphasis, always the teacher, she repeated her concern with the English translation, "What's wrong with you? Have mercy on me!"

Ignoring my mother's pleas, "Mom, I gotta go!"

I beat a hasty retreat from the house, in the wake of a barrage of Yiddish phrases-a few I hadn't heard before. My mother was so upset that she failed to offer English translations to her Yiddish cries, but I was set on doing what I had to do.

When Harry and I rounded the corner onto Ludlow Street, I could see a crowd gathered in front of John's house. As we neared the group, we were spotted and greeted with cheers.

"HOORAY PUNCHY'S HERE!"

It had been a long time, since I'd been called by that detested nickname. I still cringed at the name Punchy, but I brushed it aside and began to shake hands. When I faced John, he extended his big, beefy paw that looked bigger and beefier than I remembered.

"Hi Punchy - it's good to see ya. Thanks for comin'."

It felt awkward seeing John and the team again, but I clasped the hand offered to me.

"Yeah, it's good to see you too."

John reacted by flashing a huge smile.

"No hard feelings, I hope?"

I hadn't seen John for almost three years, not since we had the dispute over the cheerleaders. Enough time had passed, girlfriends had come and gone, and there was no point in harboring any resentment.

"No, no hard feelings. I just came to play football."

"Great! Go on over there and get suited up," John said and pointed to a white van at the curb.

The van's door was open and piles of football equipment spilled into the street. I wasn't about to ask where it came from. I was afraid of the answer.

As I dressed, I noted that all my former teammates didn't look like teenagers anymore. They were men–older looking, bigger, especially in full football regalia. They weren't the same rag tag bunch that I had played football with years ago. There was Reds wearing *shoes* and even Buck holding a *helmet*. When everyone was suited up, we actually looked like a football team. The team split up into groups of six to eight to jam into a collection of cars parked on the curb.

"Does anyone know anything about the team that we're playing?" I asked from the back seat of John's old Pontiac sedan.

John leaned his head back and said, "They're called the Black Knights. It's a colored team. They heard of us, but I don't know much about them. I hear they're damned good. It's tough to get games nowadays, so we can't be too choosy."

"Black Knights? Ya mean we're gonna play a bunch of niggers!" Smitty snarled.

"If you don't wanna play, just say so Smitty!" John snapped back. "Wasn't I just saying how tough it is to get teams to play? You can walk your ass home for all I care!"

No one wanted to piss off John and Smitty backed off quickly.

"Dammit, John, I'll play, but I don't havta like it."

A half hour later, our 49ers' caravan of cars pulled up to the curb outside a brick front, football stadium. Above the entrance to the stadium hung a yellow banner with large black letters, *Welcome to Black Knights Stadium.* Reading the banner, I wondered what we had gotten ourselves into. The wonder turned into severe apprehension, when we walked through the entrance and into the stadium. We were greeted by a crescendo of boos and cat-calls from an entirely colored crowd. From the stands, there must have been at least three or four thousand Black Knight

208

supporters raining abuse down onto our team as we shuffled to the sideline of a beautifully groomed, grass football field.

An eight piece jazz band began to play an unfamiliar tune to a catchy beat. What the band played was a cross between Blues and Sousa, if there was such a thing. On the Black Knights' sideline, six scantily clad, sequined cheerleaders pranced and danced in time to the music. It was quite a show and my teammates and I were reconsidering our agreement to play this game. Most of the 49ers had never played organized football, which made the scene even more overwhelming.

Before we could adjust to our surroundings, the sound of an explosion silenced the band for a moment. A cloud of smoke arose from the far end of the field, and out of the haze charged a host of huge, black football players, dressed all in black. Their entrance was accompanied by the band playing something that sounded like a fight song, but with an African beat. The 49ers stared at our opponents and we were awestruck by their size and the pageantry. The Black Knight players' huge size, black faces, black uniforms trimmed in gold made a terrifying impression. They even made themselves more fierce looking by smearing black grease stripes under their eyes and on their cheeks.

I was among a bunch of tough Irish guys, guys that had struck fear in the city blocks that surrounded Ludlow Street, but I could see that they were as intimidated as I was at the spectacle before us. This beat anything that I had seen in high school and college. In an effort to ignore our opponents, one by one of us began to regain enough composure to do a little stretching and tossing the ball around. Every so often, our eyes wandered to take a glimpse of the Black Knights form several straight lines to perform perfectly synchronized calisthenics. The contrast in organization of the two teams motivated the crowd to heap additional scorn onto our team. John realized that his team was losing the game even before the kickoff.

Smitty ran up to John and raged, "*Jesus Christ, John,* this is a GODDAMN SEMI-PRO TEAM!!"

"Smitty, first you don't want to play with niggers, now you're too scared to play with a real football team. If you wanna leave, GET YOUR ASS OUTTA HERE!!

Smitty stepped back from the force of Charlie's words, looked around at his teammates' scornful looks, and muttered, "Gee, dammit . . . I don't like it, but I'll play."

It appeared that John's rebuke tamed Smitty and instilled a little courage in the rest of us. John shouted, "LINE UP OFFENSE DAMMIT AND RUN SOME PLAYS! The rest of you guys, run sprints, pound each other – DO SOMETHIN'!"

We ran a few straight ahead dive plays, which helped for the moment to take our mind off of the fan abuse and the sight of the monsters across the field.

Real referees showed up on the field in striped shirts, and Charlie joined the opposing captains on the fifty-yard line. John called heads in the coin toss.

"Heads it is – the 49ers receive."

On his return to our huddle on the sideline, John read serious trouble in his teammates' eyes. He knew it would be a tough job, but he had to lift his team's spirits.

"Gather around guys! Look guys, they ain't no bigger than you or me. Get the hell out there and hit 'em hard and they'll fall on their ass–show 'em who's boss right away!"

John couldn't have been looking at the same black monsters I was, but I realized he was doing his best to jack us up. The 49ers' kick return team ran onto the field and spread out to receive the kick. In fact, the kick return team was the offensive team, the defensive team, and the kickoff team. Reds and I took the deep receiving positions on the five-yard line. The crowd's chants grew to a crescendo as the Black Knight's kicker approached the teed up ball. The kicker's foot collided with the ball.

BOOM!

Reds and I watched the ball sail over our heads and out of the end zone for a touch back. That was an NFL distance for a kickoff.

"Wow! That was one hell of a kick," Reds said.

"Yeah, the Philadelphia Eagles could use that guy."

My number was called on our first play from scrimmage, a dive off the right guard. When the 49ers' guards and tackles lined up against their opponents, the size and age disparity was immediately obvious. John had said that they were no bigger than us–he lied. The entire Black Knights line was at least ten to twenty years older than any of the 49ers, and each one had a thirty to forty-pound edge at every line position–it was clearly men versus boys.

"Hut one! Hut two!" John barked.

The ball was snapped to John, he tucked the ball into my gut as I galloped into a crease between guard and tackle. POW! I was met with a force that felt like I had been blindsided by a Semi. Before I crumpled to the ground . . . BAM! This impact felt like a bulldozer hit me. At that point, I prayed to reach the turf before the locomotive arrived. I stayed prone on the ground beneath two behemoths that had inflicted so much pain and caused an incessant ringing in my ears. I wasn't ready to get up, but John and Reds pulled me up.

John asked, "Are you alright Punchy?"

I stuttered. "Huh? Yeah . . . I . . . I think so."

John held up two fingers. "How many fingers am I holding up?"

"Thuree?"

John's jaw dropped.

Even in pain, I laughed, "I'm kidding."

Relieved smiles appeared on the faces of the entire 49ers' huddle. They were happy that I could joke after taking such a pounding. It was two more offensive plays with no gain, a lot of pain, and a punt. The 49ers' linemen couldn't hold their blocks against the stronger, grizzled opponents. The story was no different on defense. The Black Knights opened moving-van-sized holes for their large, swift running backs.

By the fourth quarter, we were at the wrong end of a 42–0 score and the Black Knights' players had become increasingly scornful. Late in the fourth quarter, I took a pitch-out from John and attempted to skirt right end. Buckie led the play, but bounced off his block on the Black Knights' huge defensive end. I did my best to avoid the end's grasp, but he collared me, spun me around, and hurled me to the ground like a sack of potatoes. I tried to stand, but my legs wobbled and I collapsed to my knees. John came to my rescue, pulled me up, and dragged me back to the huddle.

The huge Black Knight lineman, who had just treated me like his personal throw-away-toy, followed us back into our offensive huddle.

The huge man sneered, "Man, you white boys ain't worth a damn. Ya know, ya ain't gettin' a point!"

Charlie snarled, "Get the hell out of our huddle!"

The Black Knight player laughed and strutted away for his teammates and fans' amusement. John's face turned red as a beet. He looked at me, and saw that I was still suffering the effects from the last tackle. The team's captain became more resolute than ever and his voice in the huddle was low, serious and defiant.

"For Christ's sake guys . . . get some guts! D'ya hear that? The whole damned stadium is laughing at us!"

Harry moaned, "Jeez, John, they're just too goddamn big! The guy I'm up against–he's a gorilla! I think he's old enough to be my father!"

Most of the huddle nodded in agreement.

"Maybe you bums don't care, but Geordie's getting his brains beat out. He's in college and he's gonna be somebody! Ya gotta block for him! *Block – dammit – Block!* Listen to them laughing at us! Are ya gonna take that crap? We're scoring a touchdown and stick the football up their asses. I'm gonna fake a dive to Buckie and hand to Geordie on a delayed slant over right tackle – on one! BLOCK DAMMIT"

Surprisingly, John's words hit the right chord with the entire team. They were incensed over the ridicule that the Black Knights heaped on them, embarrassed by their inability to stop the Knights offense, and unable to generate any semblance of an offense of their own. John's passionate words spread throughout the huddle like an infectious disease. Suddenly, the entire 49ers' team was energized, and I took special notice of the fact that John had called me Geordie, not Punchy. To the Black Knights surprise, a beaten team didn't break out of the huddle. The 49ers seemed to be energized with fresh legs and bounced out of the huddle to line up. There was a new look of determination in our team's eyes.

John barked, "DOWN!"

The 49ers' line went down, and in unison voiced their determination.

"HMMPH!"

John barked again, "SET!"

"HMMPH!"

The 49ers' players looked directly into the eyes of their opponents. The Black Knights' players hadn't seen that confident, steely glare all day and didn't know what to make of it.

"HUT ONE!"

John took the snap from center and made a beautiful fake to Buckie diving off left tackle. After the fake to Buckie, John hid the ball on his hip. Almost the entire Black Knights' defense, that had been overly aggressive all day, bit on the fake to Buckie and converged on him. I had taken a step to the left, as if I was going with the flow of the play. As Buckie fell beneath half of the Black Knights' defense, I reversed direction and lunged forward to take John's handoff. A hole opened up on the right side like nothing I had seen all day. Our right tackle had driven the defensive lineman to the turf and Harry had taken the defensive end's legs out with a beautiful cross-body-block.

I slithered through the crease in the line to break into the secondary. The linebackers had vacated their positions to swarm on Buckie's fake dive. Only one cornerback had maintained his position and saw that I was carrying the ball. One juke and the cornerback stumbled, leaving me a clear path to the end zone.

The sound of startled and angry shouts from behind injected me with a large dose of adrenaline, and I ran like the hounds of hell were on my heels. Fearing I wasn't as fast as the Black Knights, I shifted into overdrive and accelerated like a scared rabbit across the goal line. My momentum carried me all the way to the back of the end zone before I could collapse, exhausted, and happy. Moments later, I was buried beneath an exuberant load of 49ers. The piling on inflicted further pain to my battered body, but I was too happy to care.

The Black Knights, who had been supremely confident of a shutout, looked dejectedly on as our team celebrated in the end zone. For the first time, the crowd was silent, the cheerleaders stopped cavorting, and the band stopped playing. The way we were carrying on, you would have thought that we had won the game. In a way it was a victory, when a ragtag team of neighborhood guys could even score against a semi-pro team. On the ensuing kickoff, the gun sounded to end the game, and our team began to walk off the field with the feeling that we had accomplished something by our sole touchdown.

The same big Black Knight end, that had handled me like a rag doll and laughed at us in the huddle, came up to me and grabbed my arm. If he didn't have one of the broadest white- toothed-smile that I'd ever seen, I would have feared he was going to punch me.

"That was a helluva run for a white boy!"

"Thanks, you've got a great team – I was lucky."

As I turned to continue my exit from the field, John caught up to me and put his arm around my shoulders and said, "Punch, I . . ."

I glared at John.

"Uh . . . I mean Geordie. Harry told me you're thinking of quitting school. Why in the hell do ya wanna do that? Make this your last game with us. You don't need to play with us and get

214

your brains knocked out–quit sandlot football, stay in college and make somethin' of yourself."

"You're probably right John. This game sure wasn't much fun for me, and this'll be my last game with you guys. I think I'll stay at Penn. But . . . please call me Geordie from now on. I always hated that name, Punchy."

"Okay. As long as you stay at Penn, I'll call you Geordie," John chuckled.

That was the last time that I saw John and the 49ers from Ludlow Street. Even though John and I had our differences over the two pretty cheerleaders and the red belly initiations, I realized that John always had my back. Between college studies and work in my cousin's plant, I never saw the Ludlow Street guys again.

CHAPTER TWENTY-NINE
THE NAVY

"What an awesome sight!" I shouted as I stood on the fantail of the refrigerated cargo ship, USS Polaris that plowed under the storied Golden Gate Bridge. I looked up in awe at the massive, steel, engineering marvel.

Earlier in the day, beginning at dawn, the USS Polaris had taken on cargo at its berth on San Francisco's Treasure Island. Longshoremen of all sizes and shapes had crawled like an army of ants all over the ship, and buzzed like worker bees unloading hundreds of nets of cartons and crates of fresh, dry and frozen products. Using cranes and conveyors, the longshoremen stacked and crammed the Seventh Fleet's food supplies into refrigerated and frozen lockers and filled every nook and cranny of the ship's bowels.

The full day of cargo loading was a whole new experience for me, since I had only been an Ensign in the U.S. Naval Supply Corps for three months, and the cargo officer assignment was my first naval duty.

In June, I graduated from the University of Pennsylvania's Wharton School and was commissioned as a U.S. Navy Supply Corps officer. Weeks later, I received my Supply Corps Officer indoctrination at the Naval Supply Corps School in Athens, GA. My NROTC training at Penn and the supply corps school hadn't prepared me to be a cargo officer like the inexperienced Ensign Pulver in the movie, *Mister Roberts*. I soon realized that even the best schooling wouldn't have prepared me for the hectic loading day at Treasure Island.

The entire process of moving cargo with the manual loading and unloading of pallets and nets in 1955 was far different from today's method of handling cargo that is now moved in large trailer sized containers on huge container ships.

My inexperience and the day's intense activity had left me exhausted and weak in the knees. It was late in the day, but now that we were underway and headed out to the vast Pacific Ocean on our way to Japan, I breathed a long sigh of relief and followed by a huge yawn. As the ship cleared the bridge, I took a long look back at San Francisco's glimmering skyline that began to fade in the sun setting over San Francisco bay. Our first port-of-call would be Sasebo, Japan, and after a short layover in Sasebo, we were scheduled to participate in the Seventh Fleet's underway replenishment exercises in the Philippine Sea. Fortunately by 1955, the conflict in Korea was over, and Pacific duty was bound to be far more peaceful than just a few years earlier.

In leaning over the ship's rail, I took my final look back at the "City by the Bay" to see the beautiful bay area disappear in the early evening's mist. Dazzled by the ship's wake, still glittering from the sun that was barely above the western horizon, my eyes began to squint closed–I was beat. Thoughts of leaving the security of home and family for places far across the world swam around in my head. It was exciting to imagine seeing the Far East for the first time, but the newness of my ship's duties as a cargo officer, salted by a little homesickness, caused more than a few pangs of anxiety.

My daydreams were interrupted, when a young sailor came up to the rail beside me. One look at the sailor's youthful appearance made me wonder how he could be old enough to be in the Navy. But it wasn't so much how young he looked that aroused my curiosity–it was the sailor's sad expression. If I thought I had anxieties, it looked to me that this young, peach-fuzzed seaman was near tears and needed someone to talk to:

"There goes San Francisco, sailor. We won't be seeing that for a while. Huh?"

"Yes sir!

"You look a little down. You're not seasick *already*?

"No sir! Not seasick-I'm just *homesick*. I already miss my girlfriend."

"Yeah, I think I know how you feel. I left someone back there too. How long ya been in the Navy?"

"I got out of boot camp a month ago, sir."

"Where's your home?"

"Philadelphia, sir."

"Oh? What part?"

"West Philadelphia, sir."

"Oh yeah . . . I'm from West Philly. Where in West Philly?"

"45th and Chestnut, sir."

"Hey, that's a helluva coincidence! I lived only four blocks away on 44th Street, between Spruce and Locust. I guess we never ran into each other. Who'd you pal around with?"

"I was sorta new to the neighborhood and I didn't have too many friends."

"Oh . . . yeah . . . Well, most of my pals were from around Forty-Fourth Street, but I played sandlot football with a bunch of guys from Ludlow Street. Our team was called the 49ers. Did you know any of them?"

"Know em! Geez! You played football with the 49ers? That was a tough gang! Back home, all of us guys were scared to death of the 49ers and the Ludlow Street gang. They use'ta give me and my buddies a hard time. Any time we tried to walk anywhere near Ludlow Street, they'd push us around. They sure were a mean bunch of guys."

I smiled and said, "They really weren't bad guys. Before I played football with them, I guess I felt a lot like you did.

"When you were a kid, weren't you and your buddies afraid of the Ludlow gang?" The young sailor asked

"Listen, my pals and I, we had the same fears about the Ludlow gang as you, but I learned that they were no different than you or me. Yeah, they were tough, but really a good bunch of guys."

"Did ya like playing football with those guys?"

218

"Yeah, I had rough times and some good times playing with the 49ers, but my last game with them convinced me I'd be better off staying in college. My parents and a girl tried to convince me to stay in school, but one of the 49er guys gave me some pretty good advice too, 'Quit sandlot football, stay in college, and make something of yourself.' I'll never forget that guy. His name was John. I won't forget him and the times I had playing sandlot football."

"Excuse me sir. I've got the next watch, so I gotta get movin,' but it sure was good talkin' to ya."

"Yeah, it's been nice talking to you too. Who'd ever think I'd meet someone from my old West Philly neighborhood."

Smiling, the sailor said, "Yes sir, that's for sure," and he walked off.

I returned to gaze at the ship's wake and look up again for one last look to see the Golden Gate Bridge's outline begin to fade. The cargo ship's engines hummed and the ship's wake hissed as the USS Polaris continued its course for Japan as the California coastline disappeared from view. Again, I returned to thoughts of where I came from, how I got here, but more importantly-where I'm headed.

The End

Made in the USA
Middletown, DE
17 March 2023

26938208R00126